LET your Spirit BREATHE

Living with Joy and Peace

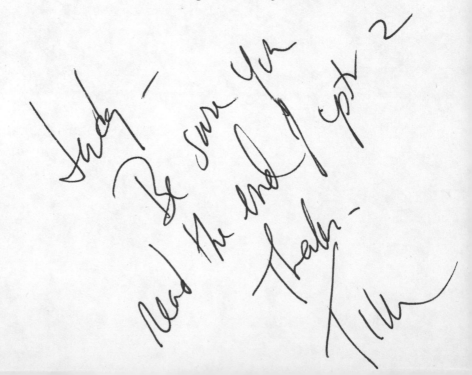

LET
your Spirit
BREATHE

Living with Joy and Peace

Timothy E. O'Connell, Ph.D.

ThomasMore®
– An RCL Company –
Allen, Texas

Cover Design by Melody Loggins, Zia Designs
Book Interior Design by Bernadette Reyna, Zia Designs

Author photo on back cover by Pete Stenberg

Send all inquiries to: Distributed by BookWorld Services, Inc.

Thomas More®   1933 Whitfield Park Loop

An RCL Company   Sarasota FL 34243

200 East Bethany Drive   888/444-2524 or fax 800/777-2525

Allen, Texas 75002-3804   941/758-8094 or fax 941/753-9396

PARISHES AND SCHOOLS:
   Contact Thomas More Publishing 800-822-6701 or fax 800-688-8356
INTERNATIONAL:
   Fax Thomas More Publishing 972-264-3719

Visit our website at **www.rclweb.com**

Let Your Spirit Breathe, Living With Joy And Peace
Product #7439

Printed in the United States of America

Library of Congress Number 99–74607

ISBN 0-88347-439-5

1 2 3 4 5   03 02 01 00 99

To
T.J.N.
H.S.N.

Two wondrous spirits:
One in our midst,
The other gone ahead.

ACKNOWLEDGMENTS

In writing this book, perhaps more than in any other writing I've ever done, I've felt like a scribe facilitating the contributions of others. Four distinct groups have blessed me with their gifts.

As you read these pages, you'll quickly discover the degree to which I'm dependent upon ageless wisdom distilled and developed by men and women across the centuries. Though my manner of structuring all this may be somehow original, the nuggets of insight are all borrowed from people far more mature and holy than I. I thank them on this page, as I do in my heart.

I've also felt myself very lucky to have witnessed so many wonderful events and experiences, the source for the beautiful stories that give life to the ideas presented here. It's been a delight to share these touching stories, and in doing so to return in my imagination to the magical moments in which they're rooted. I should hasten to add, however, that I've consistently changed details in these stories in order to protect the privacy of the people I've described. I suppose I hope they recognize themselves so they'll know my affection for them. But I also hope they're the only ones who do. In some cases, I should also tell you, I've modified the stories substantially, both to further disguise their origin and for narrative focus.

Third, in writing this book I've been particularly blessed by the advice of many people. In the very earliest stages of preparing the manuscript, I interviewed a number of people to solicit their thoughts about the topics I should address. Later on, I invited several other admired friends and colleagues to review the text. My deepest thanks to Mary Kaye Cisek, Patrick Collins,

Agnes Cunningham, Hal and Betsy Edwards, Paul Giblin, James Halstead, Bill Huebsch, Marie McCarthy, Rita Petrusa, Paul Rohde, Joseph Schmidt, and Ed Townley. The critical review and thoughtful advice of Larry Little has also been a constant blessing.

Finally, it's been my luck to have grown into happy colleagueship with my partners at Thomas More. Publisher John Sprague has been consistently supportive. And Debra Hampton has given me the gifts of skill and conscientiousness in a measure that's hard for me to believe. It's clear that this book is a labor of love for them, as for me.

TABLE OF CONTENTS

OUR RESTLESS HEARTS

It was a bright, warm Saturday morning, the kind of day when it feels good to be alive. I was out and about, as we often are on Saturday mornings, running a whole series of errands.

Driving from one chore to another, I started to make a right turn onto a small street A car was facing me, stopped for the red light. I could see the driver, a woman who was obviously a member of a minority group, and a little girl sitting next to her. The problem was that the way their car was standing made it impossible for me to complete my turn.

"Would you back up?" I called to the driver.

She stared at me wordlessly, slowly smiled, and then shook her head! I was stunned. I was angry, too; but more than anything I was stunned.

"Come on," I called. "It's such a beautiful morning, let's not ruin it."

With that the light changed and the woman drove away.

I've often reflected on that brief experience. Though it lasted only a moment or so, it remains as clearly in my mind today as it was on that Saturday morning. And many times, in my moments of reflection, I've tried to make sense of it all.

It could be this woman was simply evil, mean and nasty. We do run into people like that, from time to time. But the child in her car seemed happy and well cared for. So much about the scene suggested good people, with good values. Surely there must have been other sides to this woman.

I think there were. And so, as I've pondered the whole episode, I've come to believe this woman's reaction had more to do with the sufferings in her life than it did with me. So often, I suspect, she'd been on the receiving end of abuse from the holders of power in our society. Now, suddenly, in at least this small way, she had the power; and she couldn't resist the delicious experience of using it. Indeed, all things considered, I'm not completely sure I can blame her.

Still, there was a sadness to it all, a sense of something wonderful being unnecessarily sullied. "It's such a beautiful morning," I'd said, "let's not ruin it." And the thoughts that remain with me, after all this time, suggest I spoke a truth far deeper than I really intended, a truth that applied to far more than this brief and modest encounter.

Something was going on in this woman's heart, something bigger than me, bigger than her and her daughter, bigger even than issues of racial and social harmony. And something is going on in my heart—indeed, had been going on long before that Saturday morning—something that continues to eat at me through all the days of my life.

I call it the restless heart. And I think we ought to talk about it.

This book is for people with restless hearts. If you've picked up this book—even glanced at it, you may be one of those people. And if that's so, then this book is for you.

Let me tell you about a couple of other folks I know, other people with restless hearts. See if you discern your story between the lines of their stories. See if their restless hearts sound like yours.

Lorraine is a success—or so it appears to many of the people who know her. A high school teacher, Lorraine's liked by her students, admired by her colleagues. She's even a snappy dresser, in an academic world where most people are hopelessly frumpy. People razz her about her stylish outfits, but she can tell they really like them. And she likes them, too.

But that's all part of her outside world. Inside, Lorraine's in pain, endless, unavoidable pain. In fact, she's been in pain for fifteen years, ever since her first bout with arthritis. The doctors have suggested various therapies, and some have helped, at least for a while. But the pain's never completely gone. When Lorraine gets up in the morning, the trip to the bathroom is her first encounter with pain. The stairs at the school are a challenge, as she tries to walk with confidence—

and at the same time stay out of the way of the racing students. And by the end of the day, the fatigue she feels is so great it only adds to the pain which caused it in the first place.

The doctors call Lorraine's problem "chronic pain." It's a simple name for an awful, endless experience. No one "out there" seems to understand what it's really like; they really can't. They'll never know how it intrudes on every experience of her life, how it drowns out all the other voices that speak to her, how it becomes the accompanying voice to every conversation she joins. And Lorraine's found if she talks about her pain too much, people start to pull away from her. So she tries with all her might to keep silent about her inner experience.

Lorraine has the sense she lives in a private, painful castle. People on the other side of the moat have no idea what life inside the castle gate is like. So Lorraine lives day by day, coping with that pain—and coping with her restless heart.

It's in his car that Don does much of his thinking. In fact, the car is about the only place where he's alone and where peace and quiet can be found. So Don thinks while he's driving the car. Lately he's been thinking about his job.

Don's the director of human resources at a small company. The boss likes him, and he's well rewarded for his work. And for the most part he also enjoys it. Oh, there are days, of course. Everyone has days when there's more pressure than you want, or when the tasks seem to be an endless stream of more of the same. But more often his work is interesting and satisfying. And that's exactly what gets Don thinking.

The truth is Don's bothered by his success and his happiness. Isn't that curious? It's not that his life was just handed to him on a silver platter. It wasn't, and he knows that. In large part his achievements are due to his hard work and his talent. But at the same time, that's not completely true, either. It's not the whole story. Beyond his efforts, there's something else. Shall we call it luck? Does it deserve to be labeled grace? Don doesn't know. But he knows the flow of his life, even the success of it, can't really be traced back to him. And that's troubling. It's as if he doesn't really deserve how well his life is going, hasn't really earned it, after all. It's as if his success is not his simply to enjoy. In a way it's a responsibility, maybe even a burden. That's what Don really thinks, even if it would be hard to admit it to most of the people he knows.

Don told me how powerfully he was moved when he heard an old story about the actor Laurence Olivier. Supposedly Olivier finished a performance of Hamlet in which his acting was spectacular. He was all smiles as he took his bows. But then he stormed off the stage, ran into his dressing room, and slammed the door. Someone finally mustered the courage to approach. "Sir Laurence," the stagehand said, "why're you so upset? You were magnificent tonight."

"I know I was magnificent," replied the actor. "But dammit, I don't know how I did it!"

Don has similar feelings. His life is working, that's the good news. He doesn't know why, and that's his problem. And these strange feelings within him leave him restless, in the midst of all the nice things others would observe.

And then there's Karen. Karen's been married for twenty-one years. Her life hasn't been all that great. She's not rich, and she's never traveled much, and she doesn't have a great wardrobe. At the same time her life hasn't been all that bad, either. There's always been food on the table, a roof over her head. And there was always family love. Raised in a close-knit Southern family, Karen's always cherished the sense of unity they had. She often gets together with her brother and sisters; her mom and dad still preside over the clan. The whole family is proud of itself, to tell the truth. They're a good family. They stick together and do what's right.

That's how Karen's lived her life, too. For one thing, she's raised two kids. There've been tough moments, of course; but the kids are both in college, and they're doing very well. And through most of her marriage she's continued to work. She's a secretary in a doctor's office; and proud of the job she does, the friendly mood she cultivates in the office, the way the patients feel cared for. Karen may not be young anymore. Still, she's proud of what she's done—and she's not above noticing she's even kept her figure through it all!

On balance, Karen's life's OK—or at least it was till six months ago. That's when Jerry left her. It would have been bad enough for Karen if he'd left for another woman. But Jerry said he was leaving simply because he wasn't happy. He wasn't satisfied with their marriage or their relationship.

What does that mean? Karen looks across her life and sees lots of reasons for satisfaction: their comfort, their security, the network of family and friends. But that's not enough for Jerry.

He says he wants more, and can't find it in his marriage to Karen.

Jerry says he's tried to work on things over the years, to improve their relationship. He claims he's tried, but to no avail. And it's true he's suggested a couple of times that they ought to get some counseling. But it wasn't like there was any real problem, so Karen couldn't see what good counseling would do. To tell the truth, she thought he was just expressing the kind of discontent men sometimes do. She thought it would pass. Even now, she thinks Jerry is going through one of those "mid-life crises." And her family thinks the same.

Still he's left. And Karen? Karen hurts more than she thought a person could endure. She's embarrassed and ashamed. She can hardly face her friends. She's angry and depressed. If this is what happens when you try your best and do what's right, Karen thinks, what is life really about? I guess it's kind of an understatement to say Karen's restless. She's far more than restless, a long way from feeling joy and peace!

And isn't that what life's supposed to be about?

Do you recognize yourself in the stories of these good people? Are there parts of you that are like Lorraine or Don or Karen or, indeed, like the angry woman in the car? Does your experience match theirs in any way? Is your heart restless like theirs, whether the restlessness is due to anger or anxiety, mystery or injury? Well, if it is, then this book is for you.

There are so many of us, people with restless hearts, and we find ourselves in so many different situations.

You may be caught in a situation of quiet questioning, for example. Your life is going reasonably well, perhaps even excellently. But even in the face of that, you're not completely satisfied. You don't sense that all your dreams are fulfilled, all your expectations realized. You wonder, in the silence of the night, if you were born for this and nothing more.

Or you may be one of those for whom life isn't so good. Oh, it may have been good for a while, perhaps even a very long while; but the goodness has unraveled right before your eyes.

Perhaps you've been dealt an unfair blow. Maybe, after years of professional success, you've gotten the stunning news that you're being fired. And now you look like a failure. Maybe after years of robust and dependable health, you've been struck by sickness and suffering. For so many people, the sudden attack of a coronary or cancer calls into doubt everything they've always presumed. Or maybe it's interpersonal rejection and abandonment, or public humiliation, or financial reversals. Maybe death itself, the departure from your life of someone you really felt would always be there.

One or another of these experiences has punched you in the gut, hitting you like some school yard bully. It feels like the wind's been taken out of you, doubling you over when you thought you were standing tall and quite secure. Now your hopes are crushed, your dreams are mocked. And you're left to wonder what it means, or if it means anything at all.

Perhaps your life has been an endless path of suffering. You've struggled throughout your life with physical or emotional handicaps. For you the most ordinary of tasks have been work; and what others find easy, for you has always been hard. Or you've wrestled with the demons of poverty, trying to pull yourself out of a terrible cycle of failure. Maybe you're still nursing wounds left by childhood neglect or abuse, the secret pains that never leave and never are really undone. Or maybe you are one of the millions who, because of color or caste, language or look, orientation or occupation, are oppressed by forces of bigotry, played with by the rich and the powerful.

One way or another, the story of your life, perhaps, reveals you've been abandoned by your fellows in the human family— and, it seems, by God. You feel mocked, if the truth be told, by stories of peace and love and joy. Your own experience proves that they're false, that they lie about the meaning of life.

At times you may surprise yourself: a word of hope may rise from your wounded heart, a sense of possibilities you can't quite justify. More often though, you crawl along the path of your life with energy that comes only from desperation and rank necessity. You do it, in the end, only because you have to. You have no hope. No promise invites you to imagine a better tomorrow.

There are so many of us. Our ages are different, our circumstances diverse. We come in all colors, from all traditions; we're both women and men. And we face issues and angles that are not at all the same. But we are alike in this: our hearts are restless, endlessly and finally restless.

We're not everyone, of course. Curiously enough, some people seem strangely free of these feelings of ours. At least for the moment they seem gloriously unfettered by anger or angst, doubt or despair. For them life seems to be everything they'd like, its promise fully matched by its product. They're not weighed down or wounded.

But we're not alone either, even if we so often feel like we are. From time to time folks around us let comments slip; they voice feelings that seem exactly like our own. In moments of intimate confession, rare and beautiful moments, we've occasionally been allowed to know that others live in a world just like ours. So we know—even if it's hard to remember: if our ranks don't include all our fellows in the human community, still our numbers are legion. Yes, there are so many of us, the people with restless hearts.

To people like us this book is addressed.

You're one of those with a restless heart, and in this book I'm talking to you. What am I offering you? Two things, two important things that can help you in the journey of your life.

First, I offer you a safe place to ask your questions and face your feelings.

It may seem strange to think of a book as a safe place, but it is. We're not in the same room, you and I, so you don't have to talk back to me. You can take these thoughts and live with them a while. You can close the book and walk away when the questions become too dull—or too intense. You can dilly-dally over the parts that touch a nerve and slip quickly past the parts that make no sense. And through it all, you can keep your peace, saying nothing until you're ready, doing nothing until the time seems right. It's a safe place, this book, and I've purposely made it so for you.

And the second thing I offer? The wisdom of the ages, answers that can respond to the questions of your heart. Now, that may sound pretentious, even offensive. How can I provide good answers, when I don't even know you, when we've never even met? Let me tell you what I mean—and what I don't mean—when I say I offer you the wisdom of the ages.

I don't mean that other people's answers, even the answers of wise people, can be put on like a winter coat, without worrying about the fit. We aren't dominoes, you and I, stacked in a row, exactly alike in experience and issues. No, each of us is unique. Our concerns are distinctive, just as we are distinctive. The famous claim that no two snowflakes are exactly the same is just as true—probably more so—of human persons. So you don't produce solutions to the issues of life like you produce cookies for the holidays, stamping them out one after another. And you don't embrace the truth about human beings if you view them as identical products, all in a row. So when I say I offer you the wisdom of the ages, that's not what I mean.

I also don't mean that all the answers from of old will match the experience of today. They don't. Some of the old ways were, to tell the truth, never very good, not for their time and certainly not for ours. Some of them were infected with sexism, hopelessly tainted by the patriarchal visions from which they were born. Some of them were haughty and self-righteous, presuming a corner on truth that was never really deserved.

Others of the old ways were good only for their own time. The explanations they offered, for example, the suggestions they made were bound by the culture in which they were composed. Or perhaps they depended on scientific views or societal structures or prevailing practices that no longer exist. In any case, these views may have been well suited to their own day, but they certainly aren't what we need in our time.

So that's not what I mean. What I do mean is that we're not completely different, either. We're not so unique that there's nothing we can learn.

I recall when the musical, Hair, appeared in the late sixties. One of its most famous songs declared that, "this is the dawning of the age of Aquarius." I liked that song. The tune was attractive, and the sentiment of the lyric was absolutely intoxicating. But I remember, even as I sang the song with enthusiasm, thinking to myself that it wasn't really speaking the truth. Our age is not so unique, so unprecedented, that the insights of the past can't help us.

Rather, the truth is that the questions we raise have been raised before in the history of the human family. And the truth is that, since, even as we're somehow different, we're also somehow similar to our forefathers and foremothers, some of the answers they found may well be answers that will work also for us. By listening to their experience, then, we can profit. By observing their attempts at answers, we can be forewarned. And by attending to their occasional successes, we can benefit as well.

So if "wisdom of the ages" is perhaps too lofty a name for what you'll find here, still there are some answers that have worked for others and can work for us as well.

Those answers—and a safe place—I offer you in these pages.

I'm talking to you, then. I know who you are, even if I've never met you personally. And I understand the feelings that live in you. Like Lorraine and Don and Karen, like that woman who wouldn't back away, you carry within you a restless heart. And the dreams that seem to live inevitably within our human hearts are, for you, unfulfilled dreams. You yearn for something more, you seek what you've not yet found. Your spirit searches for what's still unseen.

Let's spend some time together, you and I. Let's reflect a while with each other, quietly and peacefully. Let's softly speak a few scary questions together. And let's see what we can learn. Let's listen for wisdom, being open to answers. And let's see if, together, we can find a key to the life we seek, to the dream that will just not go away.

Let's go in search of a life of joy and peace.

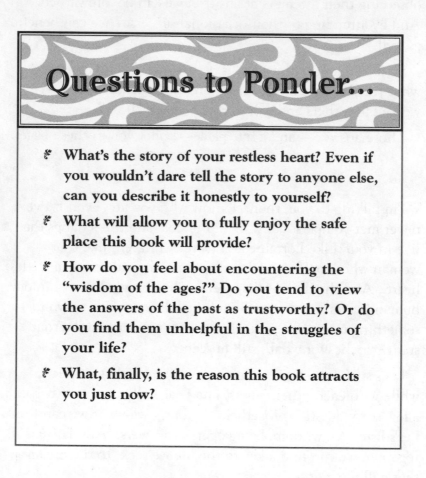

Questions to Ponder...

- ❧ What's the story of your restless heart? Even if you wouldn't dare tell the story to anyone else, can you describe it honestly to yourself?

- ❧ What will allow you to fully enjoy the safe place this book will provide?

- ❧ How do you feel about encountering the "wisdom of the ages?" Do you tend to view the answers of the past as trustworthy? Or do you find them unhelpful in the struggles of your life?

- ❧ What, finally, is the reason this book attracts you just now?

SCALING THE WALL

The sixth grader rushes out of school, diving for her mother's car. Almost before she's belted in, the car is on the move, out of the parking lot, into the street, through the town. She has only fifteen minutes before ballet class begins. She's got a problem, it seems. She's drowning in busyness, almost unable to squeeze all her activities into the hours of an ordinary day.

Meanwhile, right down the street, a group of teenagers gathers on the street corner, hanging around, not doing much of anything. They've also got a problem, it seems. They're bored. They can't think of anything to do. The things they'd like to do, they can't afford. The things they can do, hold no interest for them. So they stand there talking about this and that, watching the cars go by, filling the hours till they'll need to go home at last.

There are two great problems that besiege the human family: busyness and boredom. And one way or another, at one time or another, they both afflict just about everyone who belongs to the great human race. Busyness and boredom are very different, of course. But these two curses have in common that they feel like a great wall, keeping us from the promised land where our human spirits can breathe and our human dreams can be fulfilled. So, in order to find joy and peace in our lives, to truly, fully live, we all have to figure out how to scale that wall.

Let me tell you stories about people who have faced these walls. Let me describe the different walls of their experience, the different challenges that came their way. And let's compare those stories with the patterns of our own lives. Let's try to become a bit more clear about the various walls that have, at one time or another, blocked the way on our journey. More importantly let's try to name the wall that confronts us now.

And then most importantly, in order that we may, finally, achieve our dreams, let's set out to scale the wall.

❧

I sit in my office, at the university where I teach. I hear the conversations from the hall.

"Hi, there," they say. "How're you doing?" Then the answer comes back.

"OK, I guess. But I'm just so swamped. I'm drowning with class preparation. I haven't finished grading my mid-terms. I never get any time to do research. I'm so busy I can hardly stand it."

The first words out of their mouth: a hymn to overextension! How often we hear speeches like this; and, yes, sometimes we give the speech ourselves. Still, these words deserve some deeper reflection.

I feel two reactions when I hear talk of busyness. On the one hand, it's sad that people are suffering. The folks who give this speech experience themselves as in pain, and they feel the pain as beyond their control. They see themselves as victims, they feel powerless. And that's a sad thing to watch.

On the other hand, it really is amazing that people are surprised by this predicament, that they feel so powerless. For they—we— really aren't powerless at all. There are many cultural pressures that make it hard to set limits, of course. Employers can make unreasonable demands. Friends and neighbors can set unreachable standards. But after all is said and done, the honest truth is that we're the creators of our own busyness.

We run like rats around a spinning track that has no end, and we overlook the fact that we've chosen to jump onto the track in the first place. As if we didn't know that all of us humans are finite beings. We're not infinite like God. We're not without limits. Quite the contrary, we're limited by time and space, by energy and expense. We can't have everything. But we want everything, and so we jump on the track, run without ceasing, and then claim to be surprised at how much the running hurts.

I hear a voice of wisdom—a slightly sarcastic voice, in my opinion—but a voice of truth. "Get over it!" says the voice. "You're an imaginative person, a person able to conjure possibilities and to organize active responses. What this means is that never, ever, for the rest of your life, will you have as much time available as you have ways of filling that time. That's the way things are. That's the way they'll always be. What you have to do is let go of the illusion that you can—or should—do everything. You can't do everything. You shouldn't do everything. From now on, the key to good living in your life will be the choices you make among the possibilities you imagine. So just get over it!"

How many of us struggle to face this truth. Not just children, running from one activity to another. Also the parents who encourage this approach and who follow it in their own lives. From work they run to the gym. From the gym to the store. From the store to home to a meeting. And in between, phone calls to be made or returned.

Also generous people who've embraced the vocation of care-giver. Social workers confronting the wounds of society, clergy dedicated to the good of their congregations, teachers who love learning and love their students, too. All of them seem permanently tempted to try meeting all the needs they see. And the result? Burnout, the final toll of a life given over to busyness.

Also wonderfully lively people who just can't get enough of the riches life has to offer, activity junkies of a sort. They look at the newspaper on Friday, and begin to schedule the delights that will fill the weekend. Why see one movie when a double feature is available? Why settle for the evening concert, when the afternoon recital can be squeezed in as well? Why just play golf, when an hour remains, just long enough for three sets of tennis? Why just lay on the beach, when a good book and a cassette tape of music and a bottle of spring water can be added?

It's all too much! And in the end, paradoxically, this busyness itself becomes a burden. A fatigue sets in, and life begins to wear us down. There has to be another way.

A wise old minister told a wonderful story. "So often," he said, "people come to tell me of their pain. 'It's terrible,' they say. 'It's as if my hand is being held over a burning candle. The heat rises and scorches me, and the hurt seems never to end. And do you know the worst of it, Reverend? I pray and God seems to do nothing to help.'

"Well, I believe the pain these people feel is real," continued the minister. "But I also believe God answers our prayers. How can this be? I will tell you.

"God is a spirit, a breath of life. Sometimes, when we pray to God, asking to be freed from the scorching flame of our pains, God's spirit-breath roars into the room like a mighty wind and blows out the candle, extinguishing the flame that causes our pain. And thus we are saved and set free of the pain that was part of our life.

"But sometime the spirit-breath of God slips quietly into the room like a gentle breeze and, instead of blowing out the candle, moves close to us and whispers softly in our ear. What does the spirit of God say? It says 'Move your hand, dummy!'

"If, after our prayer, the pain remains, it could be we expected God to be a mighty gale, clearing the path of our outer life, when in fact God was a soft breeze, calling us to use the power that lies already within our grasp."

Scale the wall of busyness in your life!

～❧～

"Mommy, I'm bored!"

We've all heard that line from the children in our lives, of course. But what's much more interesting is the boredom of adults. And as we observe that boredom in others—and feel it within ourselves—it seems there are two different stories: the couch potato and the prisoner.

There's the story of the couch potato. This is the TV addict, the person who lazily fills the empty hours of day or night by mindlessly staring at the tube. There are many examples of the couch potato in our culture. They're all stereotypes, of course, cartoons that pretend things are simpler than they really are. But they also contain a grain of truth, describe a corner of ourselves that needs some attention.

There's the weekend sports freak, usually depicted as an overweight male with a one track mind. He settles himself in front of the tube, remote control in hand, and surfs between games from Friday night till Sunday afternoon. Superbowl Sunday is the greatest feast of his personal calendar. There's the soap opera fan, usually portrayed as a female with a yearning for a life that isn't hers. She knows the time of each of the shows, what's going on with all the characters. The highpoint of shopping for groceries is picking up the booklet that gives all the inside tidbits on the shows and the actors who inhabit them. And there's the hoarder of rented movies, running to the corner store for a weekend's distraction. One movie? How about five! Seen it already? Let's see it again!

What do these people have in common? They're bored. They experience the life they live as empty and uninteresting, meaningless. So they flee it at the first opportunity, replacing their real life by an imagined life, living vicariously through the adventures of the people who are on the screen.

What shall we say of the couch potatoes? Their—our—choice is sad, to be sure. I wonder if it doesn't deserve to be called insulting, as well: an insult against ourselves, against our neighbors, and, indeed, against God.

We couch potatoes have the wherewithal to fill our lives with wonderful, enlivening activities, after all. There are fascinating experiences just waiting to be had. Books to be read, enriching plays and movies to be seen, wondrous music to be heard. Museums and galleries, planetariums and aquariums and zoos to be enjoyed. There are people to meet and to get to know. Relationships waiting, friends and colleagues and fellow travelers with whom to share one's experiences and one's self. And there are endless opportunities for embodied action, from riding a bicycle to participating in a sport to, in its place, the gentle loving play of sex.

But we will have none of that. Instead, we have the audacity to announce that life is boring, that we have nothing to do, that our life is without meaning. This is a failure of imagination,

I believe. We just can't muster the energy to imagine the possibilities that are all around them. So the story of the couch potato is a story of tragedy that could easily be avoided.

Not so the story of the prisoner. For there are other captives of boredom, other millions whose life feels empty and meaningless. I have in mind the poor and the elderly, the handicapped and the afflicted. And though we may not notice them every day, we know their story well.

Near my house, the city street ends at a traffic light which regulates access to the expressway. At that light stands a wizened old lady, asking for money. Little more than skin and bones, she carries a plastic shopping bag as she limps between the cars with hand outstretched. I give her something almost every time I pass. Her need feels real to me. The struggles she faces, whether their source is a poverty into which she was born or a mental illness with which she is burdened, are obvious.

And if I needed any other motive for my tiny generosity, this sweet lady always smiles at me. "Thank you! God bless you!" she says, every time without fail. I hope my money helps her get the necessities of life. I hope my gesture, and my smile in return, offers a tiny gift of friendliness that warms her life.

Yes, we know their stories well. Almost daily I pass the front door of a nursing home in my neighborhood. If the weather is even slightly pleasant, the residents are all out on the porch, sitting and watching the traffic go by. They don't seem to talk much. They just sit, often with a blank look on their faces, and watch the world go by.

Here, I think, is a boredom without blame, a meaninglessness that reveals not the victim's failure of imagination but our world's failure of compassion. For these people are prisoners in a cell not of their own making. And without the help of others, they cannot be set free. It's a burden nonetheless, this innocent boredom, a wall that blocks the path of the human spirit, tethers it and keeps it from the flight that is our human heritage. To the extent, then, this prisoner's story is ours, we must stand like that sweet lady and ask for the gift we need, we must wait like nursing home residents and hope for the delivery of our dreams.

Either way, whether we are couch potatoes or prisoners, our boredom is a wall. It must be scaled—at any cost it must be breached—if our spirits are ever to breathe, if we are ever to really live.

≈≈≈

Busyness and boredom: they are two great walls blocking the journey of the human spirit. But notice, if you will, how the two are distributed unequally among the human family. For some the key issue is boredom, for others busyness.

The two burdens are distributed to some extent along lines of class and wealth. Middle-class people, people with substantial resources, are more likely to face the wall of busyness. The poor, on the other hand, those who have not been blessed with money or education, are more likely to face boredom. The burdens are also distributed, often enough, along lines of age.

People in the healthy throes of adulthood are more likely to face the challenge of busyness. The young and the old, on the other hand, more often find themselves trapped by boredom.

What's more, the distribution of these two burdens, boredom and busyness, doesn't stand still. It changes from time to time, with the result that any one of us can feel the impact of either of these curses. The most comfortable of middle class people, for example, can wrestle with a boredom, an ennui, that hides beneath the busyness of every day life. And on the other hand, the struggling poor regularly endure a busyness that comes from the huge, unending effort required simply to survive. In fact, the deepest truth is probably that both these burdens will sooner or later belong to all of us, no matter what our circumstances.

For most of the people I meet personally, I must confess, the more immediate issue is busyness. This is the wall they need to scale. And I suspect that for most of the people who will pick up this book, the same can be said. That's not a mark of honor, of course; it's just an indicator of our background and our moment in life. In fact, if anything, the fact that we face the wall of busyness creates a special challenge.

For if it's true that for many of us the core issue of life is busyness and what to do about it, it's probably also true that in this regard we're a distinct minority in the human family. Far more people suffer the pain of boredom, of a meaninglessness that, whether it comes from a lack of imagination or from the heartlessness of an uncaring world, wears them down and tempts them to complete despair.

So we mustn't allow ourselves the luxury of talking only about our problems. Precisely because we may have been the lucky recipients of imagination and opportunity, those midwives of busyness, we must take care not to overlook those who've had no such luck. Quite the contrary, we must try to think also about what should be done for all of us, sisters and brothers in the human family.

For our own sakes, we have to name and face the wall that's part of our lives just now. And for the sake of the whole human family, we have to think about both the walls, and to conjure ways of scaling their heights.

❧❧

"It was a terrible time in my life," Gail said, sighing as she recalled it. "I couldn't figure out what to do. I didn't know if I could ever take charge again. I felt powerless, trapped, cut off. It was like a wall stood before me, preventing me from moving forward."

Gail was telling me about the time when she abruptly lost her job. A proud and competent woman, she'd done well. Her skills as a trainer, helping other employees to develop their abilities, made it look like she was on a smooth path. Her challenges were those of using fully her gifts for something she enjoyed, something that was rewarded, something that was helpful and wholesome and good. Her plan for life called for success followed by success. But then the company was bought out, and her whole plan abruptly fell apart.

"The night I was fired," Gail said, "I was having dinner with some friends. They knew my trouble, more or less. But they weren't part of my inner circle, they didn't really know how it was feeling to me. And I didn't expect them to have any answers. In fact, the dinner was really a moment of escape, where I was just trying to ignore it all.

"But then Judy slid a small package across the table to me. 'I want you to have this,' she said. The package looked like the kind of box that contains a small piece of jewelry, a ring perhaps. But it was just a simple, drugstore box, no store name on top. I took off the ribbon and opened it. The inside was filled with cotton. I peeled the padding back, and there, in the middle, was a small, misshapen piece of stone. Flecks of paint clung to it. I had no idea what it was.

"I looked at Judy. She looked back at me, smiling. She knew I was confused. She let me hang in the suspense for a moment, and then she explained. 'That's a piece of the Berlin Wall,' she said. 'I picked it up when I visited Germany shortly after the wall came tumbling down. I have just a few pieces, and I give them only to very important friends.

"'I thought you ought to have that,' she continued. 'I thought you might need to know: all the walls can finally be breached. Never doubt it. All the walls will yield.'

"I began to cry."

All the walls will yield. What a wonderful proclamation! Even the walls of busyness and boredom–they can be breached. With a little grace and a little effort, they all will finally yield.

And our spirits will breathe, they will sail, and our dreams of living with joy and peace will be fulfilled. "Never doubt it," said Judy. And I think she was right.

The coming chapters will offer lessons in flying for human spirits. They will offer guidance in the fulfillment of dreams. They will offer prescriptions for the scaling of walls.

Never doubt it.

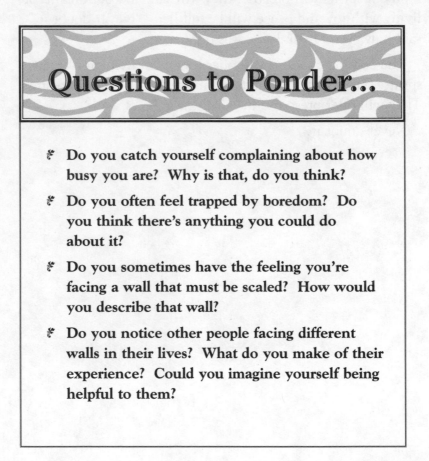

Questions to Ponder...

❧ Do you catch yourself complaining about how busy you are? Why is that, do you think?

❧ Do you often feel trapped by boredom? Do you think there's anything you could do about it?

❧ Do you sometimes have the feeling you're facing a wall that must be scaled? How would you describe that wall?

❧ Do you notice other people facing different walls in their lives? What do you make of their experience? Could you imagine yourself being helpful to them?

CATCH YOUR BREATH

I hate aerobic exercise. All those classes you see on TV, the groups of lean and healthy people bouncing around in gymnasiums across the country, the joggers and bikers and roller-bladers cavorting down the paths and across the parks around us—they all send a shiver down my spine. And I know the reason, exactly. Whenever I've tried to undertake those activities, I've been left huffing and puffing, desperately trying to catch my breath before I keel over into total oblivion.

And then I had occasion to get some advice on physical fitness. "If you're straining to catch your breath," the advisor told me, "you're working too hard. In exercise designed to improve your cardiovascular fitness, the goal is to work hard enough to sweat, but easy enough to carry on a conversation."

What a lovely thought! It's OK to work hard, but you've got to be able to breathe.

There's lots of talk about "spirituality" nowadays, lots of books being written and lectures being presented. Oprah

Winfrey currently devotes a segment of her show to "remembering the spirit." But many people don't seem to realize what's at the heart of all this interest. The Latin word for spirit, *spiritus*, means breath, from which English words like "aspirate" come. When you come right down to it, our spirit is simply the breath at the heart of our personhood. And spirituality is our name for the efforts we make to catch our breath along the path of our daily lives.

I found it to be good news that I didn't have to exercise to exhaustion, that it was alright to catch my breath. And lots of people are finding it to be good news that they can catch the breath of their lives without apology. One of the exciting things about the moment of history in which we live is the rediscovery of the importance of catching one's breath. And with that rediscovery has come also the rediscovery of all sorts of ancient wisdom about how to do just that.

Would you like to find ways to catch your breath in life? Do you think that might help you live with joy and peace? Let's consider together some of that ancient wisdom, seeing how it can make sense in our lives, in our time, in our world, today.

"It takes time to really live," said Gretchen. A wise old woman with grey, thinning hair, Gretchen has done much in her life. She married, and later buried, a man she loved deeply, sharing almost a half-century with him. She raised two children and has lived to see her grandchildren. On and off, she's pursued a career, established herself as a professional person, competent and creative. And along the way, Gretchen has become wise.

"People think the commodity they most need for life is money," said told us, as we sat around the living room of the small retirement apartment where she now lives, "but it isn't. The scarcest, most valuable commodity is time. And if you want anything in life, you have to be ready to spend some of your limited, precious time on it." Gretchen nodded, in the confidence that she was right

One of the important lessons children have to learn early in life is that they can't succeed without effort—and without the time that contains that effort. My nephew, Robert, learned that truth the hard way. He'd entered a nearby community college in the desire to advance his education. But it didn't take long for me to see he was in trouble—he didn't study! Oh, he cracked the books now and then, but he didn't put any real, serious time into it. And I told him as much.

"Robert," I trumpeted in a voice that sounded terminally parental, "you've got to spend time on your studies. A quick read of the chapters isn't enough. You've got to highlight the text, outline it, find ways to quiz yourself on its details. You've got to take the time to study!" He didn't—and his school days were soon over.

Of course, there's no cause to look down our noses at Robert. This is a lesson we all need to learn over and over again. What's important must be given time. Time must be spent to purchase the things that are really important in life.

And something more. Samuel is a sharp, observant man. He was trained as a rabbi. And although he doesn't have a congregation of his own, his whole approach to life reflects his training and his study. Once, as we were walking in the neighborhood park, Samuel asked me: "Do you know the difference between a colleague and a friend? When you think of the people in your life, do you know how you can tell the difference between the two?"

"No," I said, "I don't, Samuel. What's the difference between a colleague and a friend?"

"A colleague," he said, "spends time on you. But a friend wastes time with you!" He giggled as I tried to wrap my brain around his insight.

If we need to spend time on the things that are important in life, we need even more to waste time on the things that are more than important. And with those things that are really, finally, ultimately most important to us, we need to give time without measuring the amount, without counting the cost. In fact, an indicator of the fact that something's really, finally, ultimately important to us is the fact that we want to waste time on it and that we're not the least bit interested in counting the cost.

Everyone knows this. I'm not sure if we're born knowing it, but we discover it the first time we fall in love. Teenagers sit on the front porch for hours. They talk about this and that, or they don't talk at all. It doesn't make any difference. They're together as the hours pass by. They're wasting time, and it's perfectly OK with them. Love does that. Recently I was talking with one of the undergraduates at the university where I teach. He was complaining that he didn't have time to finish his class assignments and that he often couldn't help being late for his part-time job. Mere minutes later, he told me he needed to leave. "I'm meeting this girl for coffee," he said!

What was important to him became immediately clear! A look at our own lives will be just as clear. Find what you waste time on, and you'll find the axis of your life.

≈≈≈

"Be quiet!" said the third grade teacher, glaring at the rambunctious children in her class. They were good children, not really mean or malicious. But they had so much energy that it was hard for them to settle down. And the teacher knew an important truth: unless they settled down, became quiet, they'd never be able to learn.

What's true in the classroom is also true in life. For our spirits to breathe requires quiet. It's in quiet, when the noise of life's endless distractions is turned off, that our spirits have a chance to speak and we have a chance to catch our breath.

The Jewish scriptures contain the wonderful story of Elijah, waiting for the arrival of God. A mighty wind blew, but God was not in the wind. An earthquake shook the ground, but God was not in the earthquake. A fire burst upon the scene, but God was not in the fire. "After the fire there was a tiny whispering sound. When he heard this, Elijah hid his face in his cloak." For God was there, in the quiet and the gentleness of the breeze. (I Kings 19:11–13)

In a similar vein, there's the wonderful story of an old woman who sat for hours in her church. It seemed she did nothing. She didn't say any prayers, as far as one could tell by observing her. She read no books, she performed no rituals. Finally someone asked her, "How do you fill your time while you're in church? What are you doing?"

"Oh, I'm not doing much of anything," she replied. "I just look at God and God looks at me. Every once in a while we smile. But most of the time we just sit quietly together!"

If the quiet whispers are where people find God, they're also where we find ourselves. But for all that, it's not easy to achieve quiet. There's all that outside noise to contend with. Many of us have tremendous trouble finding a quiet place, a place where radios aren't blaring, cars aren't honking, people aren't screaming. In our world, places of quiet are few and far between. Still we do need to stop the incessant activity, to retreat to quiet, to find such a place apart, if we're ever to hear the whispers of our spirit and to let that spirit breathe.

And as if all that weren't problem enough, we also have to achieve quiet within. If the noise of our world can finally be silenced, we're still the captives of the noise inside our own heads. So many preoccupations, so many concerns. We need to silence the frantic conversation of our minds. We need to turn ourselves from being speakers within to listeners within. For only then, in the place of whispers and silence, can our spirits breathe and speak and live.

Let Your Spirit Breathe

It's fascinating the things people do to achieve that inner silence. Very few of us can do it spontaneously; for most of us it takes tricks to quiet our minds. Some people walk in the woods, while others stare at a candle. Some people knit while gently rocking in their favorite chair. One friend of mine sketches with pencils in an artist's pad, not worrying about what she's drawing, just allowing the movement of her hand to quiet her mind. Many people set aside a particular place of silence, a church or synagogue, a tiny corner of their bedroom, a particular chair. For some it's a place of peaceful darkness, a cozy place. For others it's a place of openness, a window, perhaps, that looks out on the endless vista.

I'm told that long distance runners achieve this inner emptiness during their exercise, and that they find this inner experience almost as exciting as the outer activity of running itself. I've often suspected that the hours spent by people while they're fishing have very little to do with reeling in any fish at all. In fact, the joke about the fisherman who failed to bait his hook, because it would ruin everything, catches a truth—if not a fish!

To finally let your spirit breathe, you've got to catch your breath. And to catch your breath, you've first got to find a way to be quiet.

❧❧

"You've got to be centered," the inspirational book proclaimed. "You've got to be in touch with yourself, aware of your identity. You've got to be peaceful at your core. You've

45

got to keep a calm at the heart of your being, while all else swirls around in the daily struggles of life. Whatever happens, you've got to stay centered."

This image, of being "centered," is another way of talking about the quiet we need if we're ever going to catch our breath. And over the centuries, many people have found the image helpful. I know I've often had the experience of "losing the self" in the rush of activities, in the pressure of everyday demands. Perhaps you've had the same feeling—the sense that you can't quite "find yourself," the frightening awareness that you don't know what you think or how you feel. In the midst of a day's many activities, we can be trailed by an anxiety, perhaps even a muffled hysteria, that more activities can't push out of the way.

In those moments, it's centering that will help: wise pilgrims on the path to spiritual maturity have long known this. But how is this done? I suggest a simple, three step process: stop, look, listen.

First of all, stop. Something as simple as stopping our bodily movement can make a big difference. Sit down. Don't fidget. Loosen the muscles, one by one, and then let them relax. Raise the shoulders and then let them drop. Like a car going at high speed, your body can't stop all at once. But slowly, over the course of a few minutes, you can bring it to a halt. You can lead your body to rest.

Second, look. It's amazing how easily our eyes can dart about, being captured by one image or another, distracted and

disturbed by the rush of thoughts. Don't let that happen.
Instead, give your attention to some simple, peaceful image. In
the outer world look at a candle or a picture or a flower. In the
inner world picture a safe place, somewhere you've enjoyed in a
restful way in the past. For example, I often picture a warm,
sandy beach, the gentle waves lulling me into relaxation.

Finally, listen. After all, we're trying to become centered.
And what's more central to ourselves than the breath of life by
which we live. So listen to that breath. Quietly feel the air go
in and out, bringing in the balm of strength and comfort, taking
out the poison of stress and fatigue. Feel the way that fresh air
is not only outside us, around us, but also within us. Just as a
homemaker hangs blankets and towels on the line to "air out,"
so it can be with our spirits. Let your spirit float in the breeze
that you breathe. And listen to your breath as it ventilates
your body and your soul. Let your spirit catch its breath as you
listen to your body breathe.

It may surprise you that these directions focus so much on our
bodies. After all, our goal was to catch our breath as spirits.
But we humans are enfleshed spirits, and the two facets of our
being always go together. On the one hand, if our spirits are
anxious and preoccupied, that will tend to reveal itself in tight
muscles and hunched shoulders. Any massage therapist knows
this. But it works the other way, too. It's impossible to be
anxious and fretful if the body is truly relaxed. If the body
sometimes takes orders from the spirit, it's equally true that the
body can give orders in return.

So as wise people have known for centuries, you can nurture your spirit by caring for your body. You can center your spirit by quieting and centering your body. You can let spirit catch its breath as you stop your body, look at a peaceful image and listen to your body's endless breath.

I've often had occasion to work with people who provide human services: social workers and clergy, counselors and care-givers. An occupational hazard of such people is that they can become dry and exhausted. So I often ask them, "What do you do to let your spirit breathe?"

Yes, without time wasted, our spirits can shrivel and die. Without quiet, and also without being centered, not dissipated but quietly whole. Without a spirit nurtured as it's allowed to breathe, we are nothing at all.

So I must ask you: What do you do to let your spirit breathe? Don't be too quick to claim you do nothing. This question is not an excuse for self-flagellation. If you've picked up this book, an urge to have a breathing, living spirit is obvious within you. So it's not that you don't do anything now. It's just that you still yearn for more.

Look, then, at the rhythm of your life. Notice what things allow your spirit to breathe. Acknowledge and affirm those things. Appreciate not only how wonderful they are but also how important they are in the living of your life. But then look also at the spots of emptiness in your life. Would you like to flourish more fully as a person. Do you sense that you are, at least at times, lost to yourself, lacking a center, little more than a collection of frantic activities? If so, explore ways to cultivate your spirit, to allow it more room to breathe.

Consider what you might do, gently and gracefully, within the confines of your own life. See if there isn't something you could do that would help you catch your breath.

And let there be no mistake. The invitation to let our spirits breathe belongs to everyone. This is not the stuff of monasteries or convents. It's not the private possession of hippies or new age groupies. It belongs to all of us. Look around on the subway or commuter trains. Somewhere nearby there is someone taking the time to let their spirit breathe. Let your eyes scan the windows of a high-rise, watch the crowds walking the streets or driving the highways. Among them are many who take a few minutes every day to return to their center, to stop and look and listen.

You can do the same. You can be centered. You can let your spirit breathe. The invitation is addressed to you. Accept the invitation. Who knows? You might find a life of joy and peace, the life of which you dream.

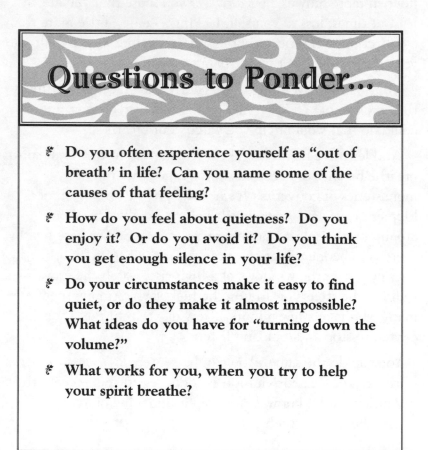

Questions to Ponder...

꙰ Do you often experience yourself as "out of breath" in life? Can you name some of the causes of that feeling?

꙰ How do you feel about quietness? Do you enjoy it? Or do you avoid it? Do you think you get enough silence in your life?

꙰ Do your circumstances make it easy to find quiet, or do they make it almost impossible? What ideas do you have for "turning down the volume?"

꙰ What works for you, when you try to help your spirit breathe?

4

Sitting in the Sun, Dancing in the Rain

I have two cats, for whom it is my lot in life to serve as a pet!
I realize the world's divided into cat lovers and dog lovers, and I
have no intention of taking sides—especially since I enjoy
both. But I do want to tell you about my cats, Duke and Ruby.
They're both entrancing animals, and I'm very fond of them
both. But they could hardly be more different.

For Duke, the greatest of life's joys is to sit in the sun. On a
sunny morning, whether in summer or winter, he may be found
on the floor, on top of the bed, in the center of the window
seat. But wherever he's found, you can count on one thing.
Duke will be sitting in the sun.

In the course of the day, the sun moves, of course. That
doesn't faze Duke. He moves, too, but no more than absolutely
necessary. He'll stand up and initiate one of those wonderful
feline stretches where he bows from front to back. Then he'll

take the necessary few steps over to the new location of the bright spot on the floor or the furniture. And then Duke will settle down again and go back to sleep, wrapped securely in the sun's brightness and its warmth.

Ruby has different values altogether. For Ruby the key to joyous living is to run and jump, to twirl and leap and dash. It's not that Ruby is after anything. He's not one of those cats that runs after particles of dust or mouse-like squeeze toys. When Ruby runs, it is simply for the joy of the chase. And in the explosion of his sprints, in the ecstacy of his jumps, you can sense a kind of joy in the mere fact of life, a celebration of simply being.

What's true of Duke is true of the human spirit: it flourishes when it's allowed to sit in the sun, to luxuriate in the presence of warmth and light. And what's true of Ruby is also true of us: the human spirit blossoms when it goes out of itself, when it becomes the body, when it proclaims in act, in gesture, in movements that are somehow dance, that life is real and good. For if our spirits breathe when we go quietly into ourselves, they also, strangely enough, breathe when we go joyously out of ourselves, in the contemplative encounter with the sunlight of beauty, in the ecstatic proclamation of the goodness of life.

Let's talk a bit about these two examples of wisdom, exemplified in Duke and in Ruby.

〜〜〜

One spring Wednesday, several years ago, two colleagues and I were driving through Chicago, on our way to an end-of-the-year faculty luncheon. Heading north on Sheridan Road, we made the sharp right turn that brought us to the shoreline of Lake Michigan. The view was stunning, the sun hovering over the lake as it made its way westward, the water placid and bright.

"Look at the lake!" I said. "Isn't it glorious?"

One of my passengers spoke up immediately. "You people are amazing," she announced. "You never get tired of that lake."

She went on to explain herself. "I'm impressed by Lake Michigan, of course," she said. "But I've only lived here a year. I'd think that, after a while, the lake would become routine, that you'd stop commenting on it, stop noticing it. But you people never do. I think it's fascinating: even life-long Chicagoans never stop talking about the beauty of the lake."

My colleague was right. And I'm sure the same kind of feeling is stirred in other people, in other places, as they respond to other wonderful icons of beauty.

One time, years ago, I was asked to give a toast at the wedding of a cousin of mine. Her wedding was to be held in the mountains of New Hampshire, in an area I'd never before visited.

As I drove up from Boston I was thinking about what I'd say. Little by little the road led up into the mountains. It passed through the midst of great, tall evergreens. It slipped back and forth across a mountain stream. It moved, ever upward, into the high, craggy rock of the mountain face. And little by little, as I drove, I found myself combining my observations through the car's windshield with my inner reflections about the wedding toast.

As I recall, the remarks I offered at the wedding suggested that our surroundings were telling us all we needed to know on this special day. For they were telling us that a successful marriage includes the sturdiness of rock, the flexibility of pine trees in the wind, and the generosity of endlessly flowing streams. As I toasted the couple, I prayed that they would imitate their surroundings, learning its lessons and following its lead.

The groom's mother, who'd lived in New Hampshire all her life, certainly surprised me when later, during the reception, she ran up to me, grabbed me in a hug, and suddenly burst into tears!

"How could you know?" she sputtered. "How could you know how important the mountains are to us? How could you know they're the symbol of our very lives? So many of the wedding guests have come from other places. I never thought our beautiful, lovable mountains would find their way into the wedding. Thank you, thank you so much!"

I didn't know. Or perhaps, deep down, at a place below logical thinking, I did know. Perhaps the beauty of Lake Michigan taught me how to see the beauty of the Green Mountains. And perhaps my spirit, nourished by my hometown beauty, was ready to bathe in the beauty into which I was driving. And perhaps the same is true with you.

We live within nature. In fact, one of the wonderful insights of recent scholarship is that we're part of nature. We're not outside of nature, lording it over the fabric of creation. Rather we're within nature, receiving from its riches, caring for its needs, and giving back the gifts it offers. This is the wisdom of native peoples such as the American Indians. It's the wisdom of scientists who point out that ecology is not something we deal with, rather it's something we're part of.

Still, we are somehow different. We're not exactly like the rest of nature. The difference is that we're the part of nature that can notice and appreciate, can contemplate and enjoy, can receive and accept and cherish. We, of all the creatures of our world, can choose to sit in the sun.

"Many people want to put some worship in their lives," said the speaker, a little man, thin and bald, walking with a limp that remained from childhood polio, "but they don't know what to do. They don't know what ritual to follow, what prayers to say. My answer is simple. Do this:

"When you get up in the morning, walk to the window. Open the shade and look at the sky. Find the east, where the sun is rising, unbidden, undeserved, to shine on another day. Then step back, facing that window, and bow. You may feel a bit foolish, but don't let that stop you. Bow, deeply and slowly, to the sun, to the creation whose gem the sun is, and to all the gracious powers that bring these gifts. Bow, wordlessly. And then proceed with your day."

❧❧

If we want to let our spirits breathe, we all need to sit in the sun. But there are many "suns." The beauty that touches us and speaks to us is different with different people. So you need to identify the sun that gives you warmth.

In Chicago, for example, if you were able to stand in the middle of Michigan Avenue near Adams Street and if you could avoid the traffic rushing by on both sides, you'd notice, on your left, the Art Institute and, on the right, Orchestra Hall. They're just across the street from each other; but they're very different places. I've also noticed the people are equally different—Art Institute people and Orchestra Hall people, both impressive, but very, very different.

For some people, the quiet experience of standing before a great painting, studying its technique, feeling its sensibility, admiring its structure and its execution, is powerful in ways words can't express. If you ask them about Georges Seurat's *Sunday Afternoon on the Island of La Grande Jatte*, for example, they can describe it in amazing detail, even months afterward. They can refer to the various individuals portrayed in the painting, talking about them almost as if they were personal friends. And more deeply, they can share what they felt as they absorbed the wondrous concreteness of the work. Indeed, as you listen, it's clear that these people are seeing the painting still, even as they speak. It's also clear that their spirit has been deeply touched, wonderfully nourished by the beauty they've been privileged to experience.

Other people talk, in a similar vein, of the music they've heard in Orchestra Hall. They'll describe the final moments of Mahler's *Resurrection Symphony*, for example, when the Chicago Symphony Orchestra and its chorus climb mountains of sound and proclaim the victory of life. They'll share the encounters with beauty that came through concerts and recitals, performances of individuals and groups. And as they speak, it's clear they're not just reporting a past experience. They're actually hearing the sounds, right now, as they describe them. They're once again being touched by the warm sun of beauty.

I hear the same kind of talk at the university where I teach, when I listen to professors who specialize in the physical sciences, for example. Since I barely passed biology in college, I'm the last person to appreciate its beauty. But when these amazingly talented men and women talk about their work, I'm often struck by the poetic language that they use. What holds them bound is the utter, ravishing beauty of the world they contemplate. Even their desire to understand is not an exercise in domination. Much more, I get the sense, it's an exercise in appreciation. If they know more, they can admire more, can encounter beauty more. And if all this happens, then in the sun of that beauty their spirits blossom.

It's strange, then, but true, that the beauty that touches one person is quite different from the beauty that speaks to another. Still, I'd hazard the guess that no one fully nourishes their spirit and becomes fully alive, who doesn't place themselves before beauty of some kind. It may be painting or sculpture or architecture, music or poetry or dance. It may be the miracles of organic chemistry or human anatomy or the great, vast solar system. But beauty is part of a life that's fully human, of a spirit that knows how to breathe. Beauty is the sun that warms the human spirit.

Do you remember the wonderful scene from which the movie, *Singing in the Rain,* got its name? There was Gene Kelly, dancing down the street, twirling around his umbrella, jumping into the puddles at his feet, flying up onto the fire hydrant and then back onto the sidewalk below. All the time, in his love, in his joy, he's singing in the rain.

I've always felt the dancing in this scene was even more mesmerizing, more magical than the singing. Oh, to have a human spirit that knows how to dance in the rain!

Recently I had the privilege of attending a traditional Jewish wedding. During the celebration, dancing played a major role. And none of the dances was more delightful than when the bride and groom were raised high, seated in chairs, and carried around the room, back and forth, until they were finally brought together in the center. Then the whole group danced around them, rhythmically celebrating the joy of life and the beauty of the moment. No rational statements could catch the truth the dancing embodied. And I suspect the dance's proclamation also deepened that truth in the hearts of all who joined in.

This exuberance, this embodied celebration, should somehow be evident in all our lives. If the quiet contemplation of beauty allows our spirits to breathe, just as much does the boisterous ecstacy of beauty enfleshed in the movements of our body.

I walk to the nearby park, a long stretch of land that hugs the lakefront through much of Chicago, and I watch the bikers and the rollerbladers and the runners. One young woman flashes by, perched on a bright red bike. The earphones on her head let me know she's floating on a cloud of music. She's also riding no-handed. As she effortlessly guides her vehicle, her arms are swinging back and forth, high over her head. It's almost as if she's conducting the music she's hearing. It's a dance I see.

I watch the local kids playing basketball. Many of them are good at the game, but one young man stands out. There is such fluidity in the way he runs down the court, dribbling the ball, cutting back and forth effortlessly. He seems always to know where everyone else is, to have a perfect sense of the right moment to take a shot or pass the ball to a teammate on the other side. There's a poetry to his movements that even I can feel. And when I talk to athletes, they tell me the poetry's in their bodies, too, that they feel more alive in the midst of this intense activity than at any other moment.

I have a friend, for example, who will describe in the most astonishing (even appalling) detail the progress of last Saturday's round of golf. I've listened to his words, trying to figure out why there's such energy in his rendition. And then it struck me. He's describing his golf game as a thing of beauty! It's not a matter of utilitarian achievement, the pragmatic search for the smallest score. And it certainly isn't a matter of good exercise or fresh air. Quite the contrary, it's an effort at elegant beauty, the channeling of vision into act, of flight into rest. To him golf is a thing of beauty, and as he enacts this beautiful thing, his spirit soars like the wings of a bird. It's a dance I see.

Many of us have to overcome our shyness, to be sure, before we are ready to dance. For some it's embarrassing to be so fully in our bodies, so "out of control," so utterly transparent to those around us. But it's still important to do. Sephardic Jews and Sufi mystics know this. Joggers and square dancers know it. Runners and denizens of late night discos know it. Practitioners of yoga and tai chi know it. Players at sports and makers of music know it. And we, who yearn to let our spirits breathe, must know it, too.

We are, after all, embodied spirits, beings who use two languages, the language of words and the language of gesture, to speak the truth about ourselves. And because that's true, spirits that are fully alive are spirits that are willing to be caught dancing in the rain.

❧

Medical researchers tell us we need at least a minimum amount of time in the sun if we're to remain healthy. The absence of our daily dose can leave us grouchy, tired, depressed, and lethargic. This, of course, is more likely to be a problem during those seasons when there are fewer hours of daylight. So the results of this sunlight deprivation are sometimes called "seasonal affective disorder," not coincidentally known as SAD.

I have a colleague who believes this research completely. She has a room set up in her home, equipped with a comfortable chair and bright, bright lights. In the middle of the winter, when she finds it necessary to rise before the sun, when she's still at work as darkness returns, she takes pains to arrange time for alternative sun. She gets up even earlier, takes some thoughtful reading, and settles down in her zone of light. She relaxes. She allows the warm, bright light to heal her soul as it caresses her skin. And she swears her daily dose of sun is the key to her ability to survive winter with psyche intact.

Medical researchers also tell us that, as we get older, exercise remains important, but for a different reason. In our maturity, they tell us, it's not strength we need, but flexibility. If we don't use our bodies, they atrophy. We become sedentary, then immobile. We start to die, our bodies but also our spirits. If our bodies continue to express our spirit, however, literally pressing it out into our physical world through graceful, gentle movement, then we stay lithe and lively and alive, our bodies but also our spirits.

Look for the beauty of sunlight in your life. But also look for the sunlight of beauty. Discover what spontaneously grabs your attention, and then cultivate that interest. Find the things whose contemplation makes you feel truly alive. Discover the dances that externalize your inner self, the actions in which ecstacy can draw you out and give you life.

Go to the art gallery, jog in the woods, walk along the streets and admire the architecture you see. Sit and listen to the music that touches your soul. Play the piano or the guitar or whatever instrument carries you to the magical place. Read novels or poetry—or write them. Dance in the privacy of your home. Dig in the garden, plant flowers or cut and arrange them. Shape clay with your hands. Find your sunlight of beauty and bask in it, learn your dance of life and perform it.

Some may fear that this devotion to beauty is pretentious, a prissy, self-indulgent sort of aesthetic interest. I've heard some people argue that this interest in beauty distracts us from the true, nitty-gritty challenges of life, from the needs of our neighbor. And I suppose such a thing can happen. But it doesn't have to. And my experience is that the absence of the experience of beauty can have much more destructive results.

I once taught in a school whose faculty was quite clearly divided into two camps. I knew I had much more respect for one of the groups than for the other, and I could describe the particular issues on which we disagreed. Still, I often wondered what really made us different. Then it struck me: those who retained a high view of their professional mission also enjoyed one kind of art or another. There was a sense of creative vision in their lives that seemed to overflow naturally into their approach to work. The other group, who seemed to me to have settled into pragmatic, bureaucratic agendas, had no such cultural interests. They were more concerned about power than about poetry. And it showed, I thought, in their daily dealings.

Of course I can't prove any cause-and-effect relationship here. But I believe it. And I commend it to you. So never allow fear to cut you off from beauty. Rather, allow the message of beauty to work on you, allow it to strengthen your spirit for service, as it will surely do if given half a chance.

Yes, find the beauty that attracts you, go with the food that entices you, the encounters that give you joy. Find the place where you will sun, the place where you can dance. Reach out to beauty, and let it help your spirit breathe. Like some wise and contented cat, let your spirit sit in the sun, let it dance joyfully, mindlessly in the rain.

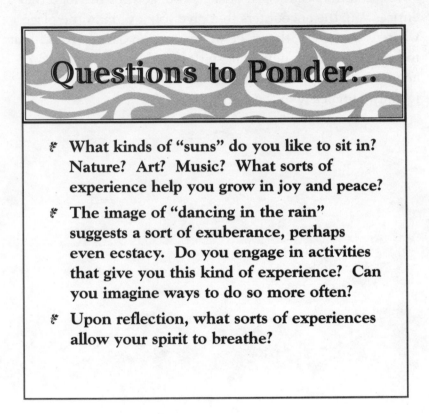

Questions to Ponder...

❦ What kinds of "suns" do you like to sit in? Nature? Art? Music? What sorts of experience help you grow in joy and peace?

❦ The image of "dancing in the rain" suggests a sort of exuberance, perhaps even ecstacy. Do you engage in activities that give you this kind of experience? Can you imagine ways to do so more often?

❦ Upon reflection, what sorts of experiences allow your spirit to breathe?

FLIGHTS OF FANCY

If you can imagine it, you can do it, and if you can't imagine it, it will never come to be.

I vividly recall the movie, *Stand and Deliver*. It told the story—based on fact—of a high school mathematics teacher working in an inner city school on the West Coast. The teacher was convinced that his students were bright and that they were perfectly capable of passing Advanced Placement calculus on their way to entering college.

He could imagine it. Unfortunately, the students could not. They couldn't imagine anything as positive and successful as that. Indeed, their picture of themselves was one that saw them without hopes or possibilities, locked forever in the current deprived circumstances of their lives.

The teacher's job, according to the usual presumptions for his profession, was simply to instruct these young people in calculus. But, as the movie made perfectly clear, this teacher saw his job through a much broader lens. As far as he was concerned, his job was to get his students to actualize their potential. And toward that end, he thought, his job was to get them to imagine themselves as winners, as capable and competent. For he knew, and now we know, that if he could get his students to imagine it, he could find them a way to achieve it.

A spirit that's richly imaginative is a spirit that will breathe deeply and easily. Let me show you how flights of fancy can nurture your spirit.

Years ago I came upon a fascinating book, *The Inner Game of Tennis*. You won't be surprised to learn that my interest in the book arose from the fact that I played tennis. I didn't play all that well, alas; and I'd often been frustrated by the ways my "mind" got in the way of my playing. I would second guess myself every time I'd make a mistake. I would tell myself exactly what I'd done wrong. Then I would get distracted. I'd imagine myself missing the shot, and I'd miss it sure enough. And the pattern would continue, as my playing spun hopelessly out of control. Given this problem, you can guess *The Inner Game of Tennis* would attract my attention immediately.

This wonderful book claimed that in tennis—and in other sports and, indeed, in many of life's activities—it's not the outer game, the one taking place on the court or the field, that's crucial. Rather it's the inner game, the one going on in the mind. In most games, it said, the body learns fairly quickly how to make the shots. The body feels what it's like when the racquet firmly hits the ball and the ball is aimed to the proper place, for example. Once that feeling is learned, the problem is no longer the body and its abilities. Rather, the problem is the way the mind gets in the way, countermanding the body, distracting or harassing it, criticizing the body's inevitable mistakes and, through the useless noise of that criticism, making it ever more difficult for the body to do its work.

Our job, said the author, is to make the mind a friend to the body. On the one hand, we should get the mind to imagine the body succeeding, not failing. After all, either one is possible, so why imagine the negative? In the case of tennis, he said, imagine the swing being successful, the racquet making smooth contact, the ball going exactly where it should. On the other hand, we should quiet the mind so that the body can then do its work unimpeded and undistracted. If the body does occasionally make a mistake, the body can learn soon enough. Don't complicate that learning process by inner shouting. Don't let the mind become the body's nagging parent. Just let the body do its job.

It worked! It worked for me in my playing tennis (though I have to return repeatedly to the wisdom of this approach). And I know it's also worked for others in many different areas of life.

I once met a man who worked as a high school basketball coach. His regimen involved all the usual tools for improving the play of his team. He conducted conditioning exercises. He had them practice the individual shots. And he organized scrimmages so that they'd have the experience of playing together. But this coach did one more thing—he gave his players a homework assignment. "Each night before you go to sleep," he said, "I want you to take fifty imaginary jump shots. Get ready for bed, brush your teeth and say your prayers. Then, once you're in bed, turn out the lights and close your eyes. Picture yourself here, on our court, and take those shots. Don't worry if you make them or not. Just take the shots. And then go to sleep."

This worked, too! The coach told me he could see the improvement, almost day to day, that came from this imaginary practice. Somehow, as they imagined it, they became able to do it. As their bodies felt the moves of the imagined shot, they also became grooved to the motions of the physical shot. And the result was that the players' success rates went up almost immediately.

The inner game was finally the key. It was their flights of fancy that made them great.

❧❦

If imagination can help our bodies act with success, it can also help our spirits breathe and flourish. In fact, the power of imagination has been appreciated by great spiritual traditions for centuries. It's true these traditions recommended the practices of quiet that we considered in Chapter 3, the activities that help us silence ourselves and become centered. But they also recommended activities that ignite and mobilize the imagination. In fact, if we view the way of silence as a first path to spiritual maturity, the way of imagination represents an important second path.

One tradition of prayer, for example, directs us to select a bible story, to reread the story as it's recounted in the text of the scriptures, and then to sit quietly, perhaps with eyes closed, and try to imagine the scene in as much detail as possible. Once we've imagined the scene, we're invited to put ourselves into the scene, allowing our imagination to place us in the midst of the event that's going on. Then we're encouraged to surrender control of the process as much as possible, allowing our imaginations to lead us into the scene not as observers but as participants.

Fascinating things happen in this process. A student of mine once shared a story of a transforming moment that came to her as she prayed in this way. Let me share that story with you.

This young woman was gathered with a group of friends for a day of prayer. The leader had suggested they spend some time imaginatively contemplating the section of the Christian scriptures in which Jesus describes himself as the good shepherd. The text of this section is well known to Christians, and images of Jesus as a loving, caring shepherd are common in Christian art. In one widely distributed painting, for example, Jesus is shown carrying a wounded lamb on his shoulders, holding its legs with the body wrapped around his neck.

As she came to this day of prayer, the student had been wrestling with a very personal question. She'd been troubled over a number of issues in her life, and had lately been thinking that some psychological counseling might be helpful. But she was also a deeply religious woman, and she worried that getting this "secular" help might somehow indicate a lack of faith on her part. It sometimes seemed to her that if she really believed in the power of a loving God, she should be able to conquer her difficulties without the crutch of counseling.

When the time for prayer arrived, then, this student followed the instructions she'd received. She sat quietly. She reread the gospel text. She tried to picture the scene of Jesus acting as the Good Shepherd. Suddenly, embarrassingly, she imagined herself wrapped around the neck of Jesus, like a wounded lamb. Her arms hung down one side, her legs the other. And her mouth was positioned right by Jesus' ear.

Still, as embarrassed as she was, she decided to trust her imagination and to accept the image it had presented. So in this strange posture she began, in her imagination, talking simply and candidly to Jesus about the struggle she was having and about the issue of whether to seek counseling.

The young woman told me that, with whatever corner of her brain was observing all this rationally, she fully expected Jesus to call her to deeper trust in God, to tell her she had no need for this human assistance if only she would put herself in God's hands. But that's not what happened. The young woman, in the silence of her imagination, finished her tale of woe, her heartfelt naming of the pain she felt, her need for help. Suddenly Jesus, this good shepherd, turned his head, looked up at the woman's face right in front of him and began to speak.

"What do you think I'm supposed to do?" he asked. "I'm not a vet. If you need a vet, get a vet! I can't do everything, after all. I'm only the Good Shepherd. Get a vet, if you need it! I have no problem with that."

Even in her telling to me of the story, the young woman couldn't help laughing at the silliness of it. But woven into that silliness was an astonishing quantity of wisdom, a wisdom that for her was truly life-changing and life-giving. And what I think is really amazing is that for this suffering woman the wisdom was utterly unexpected. In that moment of imaginative insight, unpredicted and uncontrolled, a logjam in her life was broken, her world view was subtly but powerfully changed, and she was set quite free.

The great spiritual traditions believe that the imagination is a privileged pathway to life's deepest truth, that flights of fancy are really flights of grace. Those who seek to be whole, then, would do well to set loose the energy of imagination, to see where it will lead, and to hear what it will say.

◦◦◦

The night was cold, clouds blocked out the moon's light. The day had been all too short, with dusk coming before the chores had been completed. It was, to tell the truth, a frightening time. In this fearful evening the group gathered around a campfire. The roaring blaze warmed their bodies, its glow helped cheer their spirits. Still, the mood was somber.

But then the shaman began. Softly, in a voice pitched somewhere between speech and song, he told again the great tale.

He spoke of their leader, the founder from whom they'd all descended. He described the great journey that had taken this hero from the place of his birth to this land of new opportunity. He listed the fearsome struggles through which the leader had passed, the difficulties over which he'd prevailed. Then, in gentle tones, the shaman reminded his listeners that their hero had brought them to this place and established them on this land. They had prospered here, though not without struggles of their own. But they had survived, as their leader had promised they would. In the same way, concluded the speaker, the challenges of the present moment would someday pass and a better time would come. For that was their destiny, written in their leader's deeds and words.

The listeners hung on the shaman's every word. As their eyes gazed blankly at the fire, they saw it all. They pictured the craggy mountains of their founder's place of birth. They conjured the forests he'd entered, the streams he'd crossed. They felt as their own the hard, pebbled floors of the caves where the hero had slept. And they followed, in their mind's eye, the journey to the final place of rest and hope and renewal.

Yes, they saw it all. Their imaginations had taken the lead. And living the events of the story in their imaginations, they felt the excitement and experienced the victory. So now they felt also the final peace.

One by one the members of the group got up from their places. They walked quietly to the tents that were their home. And they went peacefully, gently, safely to sleep.

How wonderful stories are! They engage the movie projector of our minds. They empower our imaginations. And in so doing, they give us wonderful, privileged experiences, transforming experiences that set our spirits free.

Think, for example, of the stories we tell one another, stories through which we share the experiences of our lives. "What was it like?" the reporter asks the survivor of the internment camp. The reporter isn't seeking information; the reporter wants to share in the experience, to feel it, somehow appreciate it, learn from the lessons it provides. So the survivor responds, begins to describe the place, the people, the events. The movie projector in our minds is engaged. We see the scene. Through the kindness of the narrator, the experience becomes also partly ours. And our spirits are touched and transformed as surely was the spirit of the one who was there.

Think also of the stories which come to us through the hands of artistic creators. Generations of young people have gained important lessons about racial tolerance by meeting Atticus Finch in Harper Lee's wonderful novel, *To Kill a Mockingbird*, or in the movie of the same name where Gregory Peck incarnated this character. Other people speak of being changed forever by John Steinbeck's *Of Mice and Men* or by the movie *The Deerhunter* or the play *Equus*.

The point is that artists mine the rich ore of their own imaginations, creating worlds that are utterly real in the way their characters behave and respond. These worlds are quite concrete, of course, with their own locale and situation and events. But for all that, in their inner truth these worlds offer something truly universal. So the artists present these worlds to our imaginations, turning on that movie projector within us. As we imagine them, we are allowed to experience them. And as we experience them, we are changed, our spirits are deepened and purified, chastened and built up. Our spirits breathe, and we become much more fully alive.

Think, finally, of the stories of which you are a part. Scholars say that, to make the story of one's life really complete, one must situate oneself within a larger, greater story. What does this mean?

It means that one of the great challenges of our lives is to tell our own story. Who am I? What am I about? And doing this involves several steps. First, we tell the story of our days, and in doing that we shape the events, situate them, form them into an overall script that has beginning, middle, and end. We make of the thousands of bits of our lives a single, complete thing, a life. Second, in telling this story, we inevitably locate it within a larger story of life. What's life all about? How do we identify a successful life when we see it? For by doing this, we're able to see our life as being part of something worthwhile. Finally, in naming our life, we also assign ourselves a role. And this role gives meaning to everything we do.

The Canadian author, Robertson Davies, wrote a wonderful novel entitled *Fifth Business*. It's written in the first person singular by a school teacher who's recently retired. The school teacher knows that many people think him the fool, see his life as small and meaningless, empty and without impact. But he sees it otherwise. The narrator explains that in many great works of art we find not only the four typical key characters: hero and heroine, troublemaker and friend (soprano, tenor, bass, and alto in the typical opera!). We also sometimes find a fifth character, a person who has a small role, but a person who, had they not been there, nothing of the main story would ever have happened. Such a character, it seems, is called the "fifth business." This, says the narrator, has been his role; and great events have happened as a result..

In a similar way, when we tell the story of our lives, at least to ourselves but hopefully to another, we name our role. Against the backdrop of some great story of life, we identify what we are up to. In doing this, we become in a much deeper way the authors of our own lives. We take on authority (author-ity) in our lives. And when that happens, our spirits breathe as only free spirits can.

Such is the power of stories, flights of fancy created, shared, and experienced.

People of spirit, then, are people of stories. They have stories to tell, stories that are always wonderful to hear. And they have fed at the table of stories, allowing their imaginations to nourish them in the living of what the stories describe. For them, flights of fancy are precious and wonderful gifts.

What are the stories that nourish your spirit? All of us have stories of our families and tribes. Sometimes they're stories of our immediate families, stories of great grandparents riding in the bowels of the tall ships, risking their very lives in the search for a new life in a new world, stories of grandparents cutting the great expanse of the new world in covered wagons, stories of parents, enduring the endless demands of two jobs to pave the way for a better life. What are your stories?

Sometimes they 're stories of our races and ethnic groups. The movie, *Beloved*, based on the novel by Toni Morrison and brought to the screen by Oprah Winfrey, presents the fearsome story of America's black slaves. It unveils the degradation and horror. But it also proclaims a victory of determination and courage. It tells a story African Americans can embrace and feel. It gives strength. What are your stories?

The great stories of our religious traditions are powerful sources of food for our spirits. The stories of Abraham and Jesus. The stories of Siddhartha and Mohammed. These are not mere collections of facts, nor even compilations of memories. They are experiences in which we share, as we hear and imagine and experience what the stories so beautifully recount. And if the stories seem to us to speak life's truths, it's because in our imaginative experiences we encounter truth, find it and feel it as our very own. What are your stories?

There's an important lesson here for those who hope to live lives of joy and peace. What are your stories? Did you once own some stories that have slipped away? Reclaim them, if you can. Are there stories that feed your spirit right now, perhaps without even being noticed? By all means notice it's so, and affirm these stories as your own. Do you feel a hunger for stories that can feed you? Go looking for them without delay. Do you have stories that can capture the flights your spirit has taken? Tell those stories. Without pretension and without fear, tell those stories. And thereby allow others to use their imaginations and so to share those experiences of yours.

People of spirit have flights of fancy. And in those fancies, their spirits take flight into joy and peace, on magical, life-giving wings.

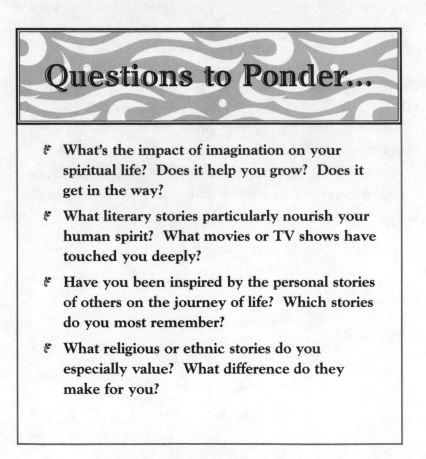

Questions to Ponder...

❦ What's the impact of imagination on your spiritual life? Does it help you grow? Does it get in the way?

❦ What literary stories particularly nourish your human spirit? What movies or TV shows have touched you deeply?

❦ Have you been inspired by the personal stories of others on the journey of life? Which stories do you most remember?

❦ What religious or ethnic stories do you especially value? What difference do they make for you?

THE PATH CALLED PEOPLE

It was a quiet evening, a chance for me to celebrate with Ken and Rachel.

I'd known both of them for several years. Actually, I'd known Ken for about a decade, and I'd met Rachel almost as soon as they started dating. I'd been present at their wedding and offered a toast at their reception. Now their first baby had been born, and it was time for a celebration.

It was a gentle celebration, to be sure. Rachel had an ear tuned to any cries that might come from the bedroom. And midnight feedings had worn down both of them. But we enjoyed our dinner nonetheless, and a glass of wine; and we talked of many things. Now, it was time for me to be gone.

"Do you have a minute more?" asked Ken, "I'd like you to bless our baby." He went on to explain, " I know about the ancient tradition of fathers blessing their children, and I like that idea. My dad's blessed Leon, and so has Rachel's dad.

You're not actually our father, but you've shared so much with us along the way. I'd like our baby to have your blessing, too."

We stood by the crib, the three of us, holding hands. I spoke whatever words I could, praying a good and happy and blessed life for this child. And a tear slipped out of the corner of my eye. A beautiful moment. A beautiful idea. A beautiful baby.

The awe people inspire, when you really look and see!

❧❧

Here's an intriguing idea. For hundreds of years wise people have written about the invitation to become fully human, to let our spirits breathe, to embark on a spiritual journey that will take us to the heights for which we yearn. In their writings these wise folks have described the goal, and they've suggested paths to follow to achieve that goal.

Many of these authors recommended the practice of going within, of becoming quiet, wasting time in the presence of reality, of centering oneself through withdrawal from the busyness of life. Many of them have also talked about the contemplation of nature, allowing the beauty of earth and sea and sky to work their magic. Or about attention to artistic creations, allowing oneself to be moved and deepened through the magic of these objects. Or about the enactment of imagination through story.

But something's been missing in these proposals. I don't claim to be a spiritual master, not by a long shot. So I don't say something's missing from their proposals simply because of my own personal experience. Rather, I've watched other people, holy and wonderful people, whom I've encountered through the years of my life. And their experience has finally convinced me something's missing from these traditional suggestions. An important path to human wholeness has been overlooked. That path is the path called people.

For example, I know several people, otherwise quite different, who share in common that they're parents. And as I've watched them, it's become clear to me that parenting is precisely what's made them fully human, fully alive. I know these people well. I've shared their lives, I've listened to their stories, I've observed their struggles. These people are holy. They have a full spirituality which has, indeed, made them whole. And what nourishes this spirituality more than anything else is their love for their children.

And I know several people, otherwise quite different, who share in common a zest for living that's centered on the people they daily encounter. Even if they're not married, or don't have children, it's the network of relationships with the women and men around them that gives their life meaning and let's their spirit breathe. It's the focus of their presence to these people that nourishes their search for a life of joy and peace. There's a spirituality to their lives I can't help but notice.

To be honest, my observation of these people has long perplexed me. It was so obvious that they were holy and wholesome people, possessed of a spirituality as genuine as any. But as best I could tell, they didn't make regular use of the paths described by the great spiritual masters of history, the paths I've talked about in the last several chapters of this book. What should I make of this?

I couldn't bring myself to claim these people were spiritually deficient. Even when some of them tried to say that, to belittle the richness of their inner lives precisely because they weren't following the traditional paths, it didn't seem that way to me. The evidence was just too clear to me: they were holy and wholesome people. What could the answer be? Eventually it became clear to me. The answer is the path called people.

In fact, so clear has this become that I now have a new, different question to consider: Why have the spiritual traditions so easily overlooked this path? We can't tell for sure, of course. But I suspect part of the reason is that so few of the valued spiritual writers of the past were married people, people whose very existence is built on the foundation of a relationship to another. Of course, these spiritual masters had relationships, as all persons do. And dealing with the challenges of those relationships played its part in their spiritual journey, as it does for all of us. Still, one way or another they were essentially solitary persons. Many of them were monks and nuns, for example, and whether they were Christians or Hindus or Buddhists, their approach to life was that of the solitary. So the paths they followed, and the paths they taught to others, were the paths of solitary life. They built their relationships upon the foundation of a spirituality already formed, rather than the other way around.

My married friends, however, are put together quite differently. They—and other people who live a similar lifestyle—seek the same goal as these saints of old, and my observation tells me they've often achieved the same goal. But the evidence suggests their path to the goal is very different. It's the path called people. They build their spirituality upon the foundation of relationships already established, rather than the other way around.

Let me show you what I mean.

It was a Wednesday, early in December; and obviously something very unusual was happening to Joanne. Her usual style at the office was friendly and outgoing, but it was also calm and unflappable. Today was very different. She was wearing an effervescent green outfit stylishly matched to her red hair. She'd applied more makeup than usual. And most noticeably, she was bubbling and bouncing like a little child.

Ah, that's it! Like a little child! Today Joanne was taking daughter Bonnie, her youngest, to see the Christmas decorations in downtown Chicago. They'd walk Michigan Avenue, they'd check out the windows of the various stores. And then, as the pinnacle of the experience, they'd have lunch in Marshall Field's Walnut Room, with its tables filling the high atrium and surrounding the great, uniquely decorated holiday tree.

Lunch by the Tree—it was a tradition for Joanne. She'd taken each of her children, in turn. And the event never failed to touch her heart and lift her spirit.

Then there's the time I was sitting across the dinner table from Melissa and Loren.

A deeply proud Jewish couple, it had grieved them when they found difficulty in having children. But after much thought, they decided that sharing their love with a next generation was more important than any genetic passing-on, so they adopted David. An adorable, outgoing boy, he knows clearly his complex heritage, and he's proud of it. His Samoan features catch your eye, as you scan the boys in the Bar Mitzvah class. But he sees no reason to apologize. Nor do Melissa and Loren. The love at the center of their family is what counts. When Melissa did become pregnant to the surprise of doctors, it only widened the circle of their love. Now, both David and Jennifer bask in its light.

So here I am, sharing dinner with this family. We get talking about the challenges of parenting. "You have to deal with both togetherness and separation," says Melissa. "At first, David hated going to preschool. I noticed that other mothers handled the crying either by just walking away, or by taking the child home. I decided there had to be a better way.

"I told David that his job was to learn new games we could play after he came home. And as I left, I had him stand at the window so he could wave goodbye to me. We would throw kisses back and forth as I walked to the car. The teacher told me I was the only mother who tried that, and David was the only child who moved comfortably right into the activities. I thought it was just showing love."

It wasn't just a dinner I shared with Melissa and Loren. I had the sense I was on holy ground.

And I think of Bill and Tom, who live on the next block. They're cheery people, good neighbors, involved citizens. They've been together about fifteen years, from what I understand, and they've lived in that house for over a decade. They've made important contributions to many community projects and offered their help in several times of need. Last year, Bill, who's a lawyer, even ran for public office. He didn't win, but I suspect he'll be back to try again. But what amazes and inspires me most of all is the children.

Five years ago Bill took in a handicapped baby for foster care. They cared for her for a couple of years. Finally, he adopted her; they'd found that parenting suited them. There are now three children. Each has a different racial composition, all of them have special needs.

I see Bill and Tom out for a summer's walk, two kids running and playing along the way, taking turns at pushing the stroller with Number Three safely strapped in. I don't know these men well, but I sense their generosity and love. "I never knew anyone like them before," said Gail, who lives next door to me. "I first met them when we took turns driving the kids to soccer. Now we share parenting chores all the time. You can always count on them!"

I suppose the path called people has many versions. But the most powerful, it seems, is the version that leads to children. Contemplating children reveals a beauty we rarely otherwise see. And loving children purifies our hearts as almost nothing else can ever do.

What's a family? A system for producing the next generation? A locale for interpersonal relationships? No, I think family is a school for the spiritual life.

❧

Children aren't the only examples of the path called people.

Dan and Enid live just around the corner from me, still in the house where they raised their six children. Now they're empty-nesters, but that hasn't turned them into sadness.

I saw Dan the other day. "What, haven't you retired yet?" I asked.

"No. Why should I?" he answered. "I'd just end up filling my time with something I love less than what I do at work. And Enid sure doesn't want me under foot all day!"

I can tell he's joking. For almost a half century these two have been together. There've been plenty of heartaches, of course. It was tough when they had to bring their daughter back home, with her baby, after her husband left. But they pitched in with an extra, unexpected round of parenting. Then, when Dan had his heart attack and when Enid had her knee surgery, there were moments of deep anxiety. But for the most part, they continue to smile, to laugh, to so obviously enjoy one another. They're the talk of the neighborhood. We peek out our windows to spy on them walking down the street, hand in hand. And we smile.

I also smile when I encounter Ruthie. She, Mike, and their family live in the next block. I often see Mike out walking the dog, and his friendly greeting is a bright touch. But Ruthie's the one who really catches my attention. She works as a crossing guard at the school on the next block. To drive by and to watch her at work is to taste the path called people.

With a vibrant personal style, Ruthie moves back and forth across the street, blowing her whistle, waving her hand. And given half a chance, she'll engage in some wonderful sassy repartee, expressing the zest of her African American cultural style. It's friendly, the mood she creates, saying "good morning" to all the folks walking along. But it's also no-nonsense. No one's going to get hurt on her beat if she can help it. The children are going to get to school. The grown-ups are going to make their bus so they can get to work. The cars are going to wait their turn and take their time. With a smile and with endless energy, Ruthie is going to make her corner a place of light and life.

I see Ruthie and I feel safe. I sense the world as a place of love. And when she sends me on my way with her usual, "Take care. God bless you!" I know she means it.

And then there's Arthur. He was bigger than life, a jolly bear of a man. But he was also a person of amazing sensitivity.

A friend of mine happened to catch a quiet example of this. It took place at a wedding reception. The bride's parents were divorced, and the father had remarried. The bride's mother was also present, but she wasn't in the role of hostess. At one point, Arthur looked across the room and saw this lady sitting alone, looking isolated and a little sad. Immediately he strolled to her table. "Like to dance?" he asked. She did.

My friend just happened to be looking in that direction, or he never would have known of Arthur's kindness. But it was the kind of thing he was always doing. And the wonderful thing? For Arthur, this sort of action never seemed to be work. It was the natural outpouring of his generous, people-cherishing heart.

Arthur lived on the path called people. And it led him to a beautiful spiritual maturity. When he died suddenly, we all felt the world was a poorer place for his absence.

Yes, so many people have found the path called people. Their romance with life and with one other, and their generous giving of care for children—you can tell they've found God along the way.

What of the rest of us? I believe the path called people can be valuable for all of us, whether we're married or not, whether we have children of our own or not. It just takes some looking and some thought.

Have you held a baby in your arms? Have you looked with wonder at this tiny living thing, with those delicate fingers and toes, those chubby cheeks? Have you felt the sacredness of that moment, the sense of a holiness that's never far away? If so, then you know the path called people.

Have you gone to a public park on a warm and sunny day? Have you watched the mothers wheeling the buggies with the little toddlers strapped safely inside? Have you, perhaps, seen one of those adapted buggies parents can push as they jog along the path? Or the very different buggies that can be attached behind a bicycle? Have you watched the slightly older children run about, playing on the swings, chasing one another in games whose rules only they know? Have you listened to their giggles, their shouts of joy? Have you smiled yourself when the inevitable tears make their appearance from time to time? If so, then you know the path called people.

Have you stood quietly, biting your lip, as teenagers whom you once knew as toddlers donned their gowns and tuxedos, off to their first prom? Have you watched them cross the stage at graduation? Have you waved them off to college, seen them climb on the bus to boot camp? Have you witnessed the magical moment when two young people exchange the vows that place them decisively on the path called people? If so, then you know that path, as well.

Have you been the recipient of those magic words that can never be forced from another human being? Has someone said, "I love you!"—someone who really knew and therefore perhaps had every reason not to love you? Has someone said "I forgive you!" when you weren't sure you really deserved forgiveness? If so, then you know the path called people.

Have you given love, in that same, very free and willing manner? I remember being moved by a scene in the movie,

Marvin's Room. One sister, grumpy at this intrusion upon her life, returns to the family home where her sister has been caring for their elderly father. The second sister explains her surprising contentment by the fact that she's been lucky in love. "Yes, you have," says the first sister. "You've always been loved." The second sister looks at her with puzzlement. "I didn't mean the love I've received. I meant the love I've been lucky enough to give. I've had such wonderful opportunities to love." The grumpy sister is stunned into silence. But if you know what this woman meant, if you feel lucky in the love you've been able to give, then truly you know the path called people.

≈≈

Yes, you know the path called people; so do we all. And if we know that path, we, all of us, should cultivate that path. For the path called people is, perhaps more than any other path, the way that will lead ordinary people of our time to the goal that our hearts finally seek, a spirit that breathes, a life lives with joy and with peace.

But how do we do that? How do we go about cultivating the path called people? It's not enough, after all, just to be around people. The other day I was driving home from downtown Chicago, cruising along at a reasonable pace on Lake Shore Drive, our beautiful highway by the water. Suddenly, on my right a car rushed past me. The driver swerved in front of me, slipped between two cars, cut again to the right, and then accelerated into the distance.

The driver was breaking the speed limit, of course. But what most struck me was not the legalities of the matter, or even the issues of safety. I found myself wondering what his hurry was! If he was on his way to a hospital, or to a critical meeting, I suppose I could understand his rush. But nothing gave me any indication this was the case. Quite the contrary, I had the feeling he was just rushing for the challenge of it. To him, the other people were not fellow travelers on life's journey. They were enemies, competitors to be outsmarted, outdistanced, and finally outdone. This man was near many human persons. But he certainly wasn't on the path called people.

Nearby people, after all, can be either friend or foe. And to cultivate the path called people, we have to see people as friends. How can we do that?

"Look me in the eye, you varmint!" said the cowboy in the old black-and-white movie. "Look me in the eye." I think that's how we see people as friends—or at least how we start to do that. And thus, it's how we cultivate the path called people. For when you look someone in the eye, you see, at least in a glimmered way, the soul. You sense the depths of the person, you feel the mystery at the core. You feel the awe that persons can prompt. And that awe, accepted and received and embraced, is the heart of this path.

Recently I had occasion to visit the office of an acquaintance, a professional person. The walls were lined with large photographs, almost all of them close-ups of faces. The people in the pictures were from all parts of the world, men and women, young and old. I inquired, "How do you get these pictures? They seem so natural. Do you photograph these people surreptitiously, from a distance?"

"No," she responded. "I want to catch the essence of their selfhood, and that feels to me like something of an intrusion. So I wouldn't feel right photographing them without their permission. I simply ask them if I can take their picture. Then, as they stand relaxed and natural, I snap my photos."

That's it! Through a camera—or through the camera of our own sight—look people in the eyes. With respect and interest look at them. And accept what you see: the mystery, the wonder, the joy and pain, the insight and uncertainty you see. Embrace it within yourself. Honor it. Allow it to touch you and transform you. Allow it to teach you. And then walk on with the gift of that learning.

You will be on the path called people.

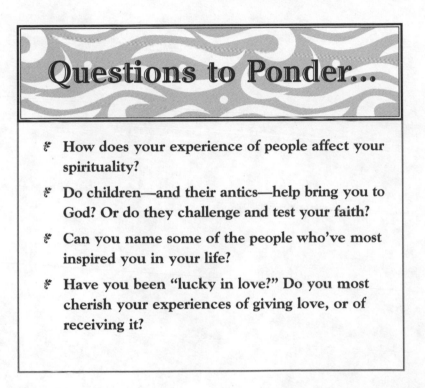

Questions to Ponder...

❦ How does your experience of people affect your spirituality?

❦ Do children—and their antics—help bring you to God? Or do they challenge and test your faith?

❦ Can you name some of the people who've most inspired you in your life?

❦ Have you been "lucky in love?" Do you most cherish your experiences of giving love, or of receiving it?

I Gotta Be Me

"What does it take to let your spirit breathe?" There's really only one universal answer to that question: "It depends!" It depends on where we are, it depends on whom we're with. It depends on our past experiences and our future plans. It depends on millions of things.

But more than anything else, maybe the challenges that face us—as we seek to grow into the persons we dream of being—depend on two things: temperament and time. In this chapter, let's look at each of these factor. And let's see what difference they make for each of us as persons.

The two people Mike described to me could not have been more different. Still, he told me that they were both quite typical of the young people participating in his program.

Amy was a lively and outgoing person. She wasn't afraid of anything, it seemed. She had a passion for serving the poor and was happiest when she was working in the soup kitchen. And truth to tell, the clients of the kitchen were happiest when she was there, too. Amy was so friendly, she remembered so many names, it was always a delight for them to deal with her.

At the house, where the members of this after-college volunteer program shared their common life, Amy was a live wire, too. She seemed deeply devoted to her religious faith. Still, she had a saucy, irreverent style that made her seem anything but pious. She spoke candidly about her faith and about how she felt God wants us to act in this world, but she spoke without pretension. She also spoke without uncertainty. Amy was one of those persons who, whatever they may someday die of, will surely not die of self-doubt!

Phil was very different. A quiet young man, hesitant and questioning, it took him quite some time to share what was in his heart. When he did, Mike told me, he revealed himself as a person every bit as impressive as Amy. He was just very different.

Phil had an acute sense of how ambiguous things are in our world. It wasn't clear to him who the good guys and bad guys are. He saw three sides of every question, and his thinking usually ended up with more possibilities than it began with. Indeed, precisely because of the anxiety his perspective caused him, Phil cherished deeply the consolations of his faith. He was a pious person, in the very best sense of that word. He prayed, and his prayer was honest. He treated religious things with genuine respect, and the respect came from the bottom of his heart. He believed that the certitudes of religion offer a bulwark against the chaos of the world, and he feared that tearing them down would leave us dangerously, maybe hopelessly, exposed.

You won't be surprised to know that Amy and Phil didn't get along. And yet, according to Mike, they were both typical of the wonderful young people with whom he was privileged to work.

And Mike, himself? Well, he wasn't that much older than Amy and Phil, about thirty I'd guess. Yet he was very different than either of them.

Mike had an odd, wonderful combination of enthusiasm and gentleness organized around an unnerving, intoxicating smile. When he grinned, which he did often, it seemed to come right out of the center of his soul. And it was a grin of peace, not of silliness. Mike was a serious person. He'd worked as a Peace Corps volunteer after college, which led naturally to his present job. In his late twenties he'd married, and just recently, he and his wife had had their first child, a beautiful baby girl.

There was a passion for goodness in Mike that seemed out of sync with his age. But I have no doubt it was genuine, an abiding dimension of who he was.

These three young people, so close in age, were still tremendously different. Their temperaments ranged from jovial to quiet, from outgoing to shy, from confident to anxious. None of them was wrong or sick or abnormal. Maybe they'd benefit from a bit of psychotherapy; we're all less than perfectly integrated, after all. But their basic temperaments didn't need work. In fact, attempting to change those temperaments would finally fail. It's who they are. For better or worse, this is the person who's traveling through life. This is the person who's spirit is yearning to breathe. So they'd better just get used to it.

A key step in learning how to live with joy and peace is discovering who we are, what our temperament is. How we experience things, how we learn, how we make decisions, how we grow—all these are part of who we are. We need to understand ourselves and accept ourselves if our spirits are ever to flourish.

One group of researchers, for example, distinguishes between introverts and extroverts. These terms need a bit of explaining; they're not just other words for "shy" and "bubbly," not at all! A person may very easily be a jolly introvert or a quiet extrovert. Rather, the terms indicate the primary source of a person's energy. Introverts find energy within themselves, while interacting with other people costs energy. Extroverts, on the other hand, find energy in their connections with other people, while looking within and attending to themselves as individual beings spends and depletes their energy.

Everyone needs both to engage in personal reflection and to interact graciously with others, of course. So these terms don't give us an excuse to cultivate only one side of ourselves. But they do help us understand why some experiences are deeply energizing while other experiences take some work. And they also help us understand how we need to proceed, in order to help our spirits flourish.

"I used to have such trouble praying," the wise old lady told me. A grandmother several times over, her life was rich with experiences and activities. "When I looked in books for advice," she went on, "they offered very detailed instructions. But no matter how much I tried, I just couldn't follow them. The instructions said they were providing a method for thinking about things, but I couldn't even figure out what that meant. I'm always thinking; I don't know how not to think!

"And then I realized. Those instructions were designed to help extroverts with the tough work of thinking. I'm an introvert. For me, those instructions only got in the way. I just needed to give myself permission to enjoy the experience of being quiet, of going within. Once I did that, once I let go of all the instructions, everything was fine!"

That lady was so wise. She knew herself, so she knew what she needed to do. So also did another wise old woman that I heard about. She was a nun, a member of a community of nuns in a cloistered convent, spending their lives in dedicated prayer.

One time an expert in prayer, a monk himself, came to offer guidance to the nuns. The monk believed deeply in the power of imagination, so he proposed to lead the nuns through an imaginative reflection. To help, he suggested the nuns all turn their chairs outward, toward the walls, so they could look at blank space and avoid any distractions.

Then he began his imaginative journey. But suddenly this one nun, a quiet, elderly lady who seemed quite withdrawn, raised her hand. "Yes, sister," said the monk, "what's the matter?" "I have a problem," she replied. "I don't mean to be a bother, but, you see, I can't pray if I can't see the other sisters!"

Beneath her quiet demeanor, this nun was an extrovert. And she knew herself well enough to know what she needed.

We need to observe our lives, to notice where we get energy and where we spend it. We need to understand the patterns and rhythms of our lives. We need to accept ourselves, in the deepest, best sense of that word. We also need to grow, of course. No one ever completes the journey to wholeness. Those of us who are introverts need to work at seeing and incorporating the beauty to be found outside. Those of us who are extroverts need to practice stepping away, taking stock, slowing down and coming home to ourselves. But we need to build these strategies of growth on a firm foundation of self-knowledge and self acceptance.

We are, after all, people of very different temperaments. Embracing those temperaments, accepting and appreciating them, is a key step on the road to a life of joy and peace.

Temperament makes a difference. And so does time. Where we are on the road of our life's journey, whether we're young or old, getting started or looking for closure: all this makes a great, tremendous difference.

Take Kristi, for example. She first approached me several years ago, after a talk I gave. She found some of my remarks particularly helpful and thought she might benefit from personal conversation. It was a mark of her passion for learning that she took the initiative of reaching out to me. A young woman in her mid-thirties, Kristi has academic interests that are very wide; and her intellect is sharp, probing, and bright. As we talked, I found she was full of questions— not so much questions about herself as questions about life. And she seemed to have endless energy for finding the answers. Recently, for example, she's become convinced that those who care about our world must attend to the needs of the millions of Spanish-speaking people in our midst. Suddenly the message on her answering machine has blossomed into a bilingual tour de force, as English and Spanish coexist in warm hospitality extended to every caller.

Kristi is a journeyer, on a road to which she's firmly committed.

Dick, on the other hand, is someone I'd describe as an explorer. A psychologist about to turn fifty, Dick and Jerri have raised their family; and now they find themselves thinking about what to do with the rest of their lives. Dick's work is successful, and he's good at it. But he has a feeling he'd like to do more. And in a particular way, he's drawn to the deeper questions of life. He wants to pursue those questions for himself, and he wants to help other people wrestle with those questions in their different circumstances. It blew my mind when I found out Dick has gone back to school! He wants to cultivate the skills of a religious minister, to round out his skills as a social scientist. And his age strikes him as no problem at all.

I suppose his age shouldn't be a problem. It's certainly not a problem to Janet, who recently celebrated her eighty-second birthday. Janet's an inspiring person, but not in a goody-two-shoes way. She starts every day with a brisk half-hour walk. Chores fill much of the morning, though she's always careful to save time for the crossword puzzle. She goes to the grocery with one of her friends who still drives, bakes cakes for neighbors who don't get out so often, and makes sure her apartment is clean and neat. Just before lunch, there's *All My Children* to watch. "I love all the issues of the show," she tells me. "I learn so much about people very different from me. Oh, I know some of the plots are silly. But some of them are kind of important, too."

Janet says her rosary in the afternoon, before her nap. If she wakes up in the middle of the night, which she frequently does, then another rosary fills the time until she falls asleep again. The late afternoon brings her to the news shows on TV. Janet thinks it's important to know what's going on. How would she ever have been able to complete her absentee ballot in the recent election, after all, if she hadn't been keeping up with the news. But she does. Along with the news comes her cocktail, followed by a simple dinner. And it's early to bed for Janet, to be ready for another day.

Some scholars say that different questions typically dominate the different periods of our lives. The first half of life, it's argued, is built on a movement outward, as the person struggles to achieve competence and confidence in the world. Young men and women alike, though with differences between them, seek to answer the question: Am I at home in this world? Do I belong here? Do I fit in? Am I a success at doing the things human persons do?

What things? Many, of course. Achieving relationships is one important task. Getting a job, keeping a job, and succeeding at a job are important, too. For some people the outward signs of success are important: titles and approval and money. For many people it's important to become a parent, to prove one can stand in the great chain of being not only as a recipient of its gifts, but also as a contributor. One way or another, though, all these concerns contribute to the human journey outward, where even the most shy and withdrawn of persons seeks to "conquer the world" one way or another, and so to find a home on this planet.

The second half of life, the scholars say, has another focus altogether. The situation is a bit like that of an army that plows aggressively forward, into enemy territory, only to wake up to the frightening feeling that one's home camp has been left empty and undefended. Oops! Better get home! Better attend to the basics, the inner center from which all things have grown.

So, the journey of the second half of life is a journey within, to the center of the person. It's an attempt to discover who I am when I'm doing nothing. Perhaps even more deeply, and fearfully, it's the attempt to discover who I am when all the tasks have failed, when the projects have ended and shown themselves less than fully successful, when the relationships have become empty, or at least incompletely rewarding, when the lure of the world has proven itself false, its promises illusory, its potential distinctly limited. These are the questions of life's second half. No longer is it a question of what I do or whom I'm with. It is simply and finally a question of who I am.

❦

The social psychologist Daniel Levinson has done extensive research into the flow of people's lives, as they pass through the years of adulthood. And he's found that an amazing amount of change takes place in the course of those adult years of our lives.

Many people think of change as a characteristic of childhood and, perhaps, of early adulthood. But Levinson shows that the process of change never ends for us. Two points about this change, as he's documented it, strike me as particularly fascinating. And I think you'll find them useful.

First, Levinson's found that we travel around a "great circle of change" that has several predictable moments. Let's start the circle with a moment when, after lots of confusion, we finally figure out how things should be in our lives. Perhaps we've decided what we want to study in school, or which job we want to take, or whom we want to marry. What a flush of energy comes from this clarity, what powers for action are easily released! We feel new and alive, completely whole and utterly focused.

Some of this first flush of energy eventually dissipates, of course. But it still leaves behind a residue of comfort, a period of calm and confidence. In these times of our lives, we have a sense that we know our place and our job, we know who we are and what we want to do. And in this knowledge we're able to act in ways that bring us joy and peace, a sense of satisfaction that has no need to be doubted or questioned.

This confidence may last as much as a decade, says Levinson. Little by little, however, the answers we've accepted start to seem inadequate. Little by little we sense that we're saying the same old truths, but we believe them less and less. We're doing the same things, but we're liking them less and less. We have the same relationships, but they satisfy us less and less. So little by little our personal synthesis starts to unravel.

This unraveling eventually leads to a crisis—perhaps not a crisis anyone nearby could see, but most certainly a crisis a person can feel. And at this moment of crisis, a challenge faces us. We can try to hold on to the old synthesis, to live as if it still worked. But if we do this, we atrophy, dying a little, replacing flexibility with rigidity, creativity with endless repetition. Instead of moving forward, we simply run in place. And we put a violent stop to the process of our lives.

Or we can take the great risk of life, letting go of the old in order to reach out for the new. We can admit to ourselves that the time has come for new answers, and we can set out to find those answers. If we do this, however, we agree to live through a terrifying moment. Why? Because we have to let go of the old synthesis first, before we can have any hope of finding a new one. So we have to embrace the terrifying truth that for now, for this moment, we have no answers at all. We have to look in the mirror and speak the truth: "I don't know where I'm going. I don't know what to do. I don't know who I am."

At least for a moment, then, we become a person with no answers, as we freely admit that the old answers no longer work. But if we take this risk, slowly, painfully, experience starts to show us new answers that make sense for us in new and deeper ways. Slowly, painfully, we come to new understandings of ourselves, of our place in the world, of our job and our purpose in life.

The new answers may agree with the old ones. This process of questioning doesn't necessarily mean abandoning old commitments. On the contrary we may reaffirm our commitments to a person or a task. We may embrace again the understanding of ourselves that's long been ours. But it does mean abandoning old life-answers that were formulated long ago, replacing them with new answers that, even if they are the same, are nonetheless much deeper and wiser, more fully understood and more completely meant.

With these new understandings, then, new energy comes to us. And the cycle begins again.

This is the first wonderful insight that comes from Levinson— the sense of a cycle in our lives, a movement through which we may pass three or four times in our adult lives.

The other insight is also wonderful, but in a different way. In his research, Levinson tried to find out how long each of the components of the cycle lasted. He found that a truly satisfying life-synthesis lasts about ten years. If we include the first flush of discovery at one end and the first intimations of inadequacy at the other, we might be talking about fifteen years, though it can be less. On the other hand, the period during which we have no synthesis, the period when we know the old answers aren't really adequate but when we haven't yet found new answers we're ready to embrace—this period can last from three to five years. And if we include the firsts inklings that the old answers aren't working at one end and the first moment of a new synthesis, when it's still being tested, at the other, then the period could be as long as five to eight years.

All these numbers are approximate, of course. We're all individuals, and there are individual differences in the flow of our lives. The point I find noteworthy, however, seems to apply to us all, one way or another. And what is that point? It's this: we all spend a good third of our adult lives in "visionary disarray!"

Yes, for a good hunk of our adulthood, we're not the confident and focused persons we may appear to be. Rather, we're hesitant searching selves, unsure but questioning, hopeful but also doubtful. And these painful moments are not occasional brief interludes. Rather they're substantial contributors to the overall flow of our lives.

～◐～

What's all this mean, this data about the segments of the cycle of our adult lives? I think it means that spirituality, that journey into self-knowledge and self-acceptance, is an ongoing need throughout our lives. But it also means that, in the various moments of our lives, our spirituality can look very different.

Even for Amy and Phil and Mike, the differences in their temperaments mean that they have different needs as the try to pursue their heart's desire. But at least they share the sense of being in the first moments of an exciting life-journey. How different things look for Janet, as she experiences the "fullness of years!" Many things they would consider very important strike her as distinctly secondary. And on the other hand, life-issues that loom large in her consciousness may be given scant attention by the young people.

And the other people whose stories I told you? They fall somewhere in between. Kristi is still young, but her life experiences have left her with a questioning, reflective perspective. And Dick has weathered a "mid-life crisis." Indeed, it seems he's flourishing in its shadow, as he reorders his priorities and refocuses his energies.

What's more, each of these people stands somewhere on the Great Circle of Change, in which they embrace, then enjoy, then lose particular understandings of what it's all about. Each one of them is in a moment either of confidence or uncertainty. And for that moment, in that moment, there is nothing to be done but to live.

Ask any of the people: "What's your heart's desire?" They will have an answer—never doubt it. In some way or another, each one of them will answer, "I want my spirit to breathe!" But ask them what's needed to give that breath of life, and the answers will be very different. And the tools they need to pursue those answers will also be different. Some of them will be experiencing a time of fullness. Their hearts speak a message of joy, of vitality, of gratitude. Some of them will be in a time of emptiness. Their hearts will offer a cry of pain, of confusion, of yearning. But for all of them, the voice of their hearts, of their spirits, will name their need and prescribe their plan.

The Hebrew scriptures include the wonderful wisdom that declares: "For everything there is a season, and a time for every matter under heaven." (Ecclesiastes 3:1) We know this is true. And because we know this, we know also that the key to letting our spirits breathe is accepting ourselves. The key is knowing who we are, how we're made up, what we're facing, and how we're feeling.

The key is affirming, not in a cocky way but in a way that's deep and true, "I gotta be me!"

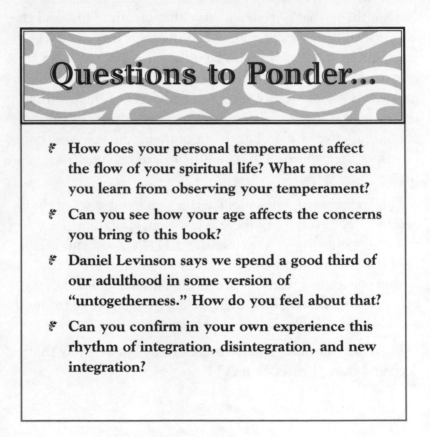

Questions to Ponder...

❦ How does your personal temperament affect the flow of your spiritual life? What more can you learn from observing your temperament?

❦ Can you see how your age affects the concerns you bring to this book?

❦ Daniel Levinson says we spend a good third of our adulthood in some version of "untogetherness." How do you feel about that?

❦ Can you confirm in your own experience this rhythm of integration, disintegration, and new integration?

No Pain, No Gain

Discipline! What an ugly word.

I suppose some people actually enjoy discipline. Every once in a while we run into people who seem to be "natural ascetics," men and women for whom control and self-denial seem to come quite easily. But most people, in my experience, hate it. For that very reason, I imagine, many folks would think the topic of discipline has no place in a book on living with joy and peace.

I understand their feelings; in many ways I share them. But, in the end, I think the topic of discipline needs to be here. So let's talk first about why we dislike this idea. And then let's see if we can find a good, genuinely helpful place for it in our quest for a spirit that breathes.

"I was raised in an Irish-American Catholic household," announced the mother, an attractive woman in her mid-thirties. It was a meeting for the parents of the children in the parochial school, and they were talking about their experiences.

"I was taught that the most important thing is doing God's will and that we must never stop trying to find out what that will is," she went on. "And we were taught that God's will inevitably involves making sacrifices and giving thing up. 'Offer it up,' was my mother's answer to my every complaint! We went to church on Sunday, stayed away from meat on Friday. We checked the Legion of Decency ratings before we went to a movie, prayed for people who bought Playboy, and never went near the YMCA. We stayed married to the same person, embraced whatever children might come, and figured we deserved all the miseries life sent our way. Then, one time a priest came into our classroom and asked us to list all the reasons we were glad we were Catholics. No one could think of a single one!"

Why do people hate discipline? It's not just because they're lazy. Rather it's because of something deeper. For many of us, the demand for discipline feels like an insult—to God and to ourselves.

For example, searching endlessly for that mysterious thing called "God's will"—isn't that odd? If God really has a will for our lives, isn't it strange that it's so difficult to find? When we want someone to do something, we make a point of clearly indicating what we want and why we want it. Why is God so mysterious about it all?

And if we're children of God, beings who come from the hand of a loving God, called to live in the love of that God forever, why's the achievement of union with God so difficult?

If I seek someone's love, I work to be lovable and I take pains to make myself available for love. Why is God so contrary?

This call to "offer it up." What sort of God does that imply? Does it make sense that a God who created a beautiful world and then placed within that world creatures as wonderful as human beings would then instruct those people to view the world as a "vale of tears," a place of suffering and self-denial? The God the great religious traditions proclaim, after all, is not this sneaky being, playing hard to get, demanding exorbitant prices that have no purpose whatsoever. Rather, it's a God who's closer to us than we are to ourselves, a God as accessible as reality itself. Shouldn't we just trust such a God of love to respond to the good will of our everyday efforts?

All these questions cross the minds of many good people. And they lead to a single, forceful conclusion: the demand for discipline is an insult.

Are you one of these people? Have you pulled away from a religion of sacrifice and denial, of demands and expectations, of shoulds and oughts and musts? Have you rejected all this talk of spiritual discipline, of regimens for personal growth and human fulfillment? Many people have.

"I'm a very spiritual person," the elegant young woman told me, as we sat side by side on the airplane. I was impressed by this woman. She worked for a company that provided some kind of financial services. It was obvious she was very competent, and the ease with which she settled into her seat had told me she traveled a lot.

I don't remember exactly how our conversation began. Soon enough she was asking me about my work. I explained that I'm a writer, trying to explore the connections between religious and spiritual values and everyday life. She responded immediately. "I'm a very spiritual person," she repeated. "But I'm not at all religious. In fact, I think religion is the enemy of spirituality."

I was a little stunned by the decisive way she said that. I asked her what she meant. "Religion is negative," she explained, "it condemns and criticizes. It harps about denial and discipline. What I embrace is spirituality, a vision of love and joy, of peace and harmony. I choose life, and I reject all the deadness that's preached in the churches."

No wonder we're inclined to flee discipline, as fast as our feet can carry us!

❧❧

Isn't it odd? At the very moment when so many of us are fleeing discipline, rejecting it as death-dealing and demeaning, others of us are running full-speed to embrace its strict demands.

Discipline is the key to physical fitness, for example. And fitness—being beautiful and healthy—is certainly one of today's obsessions. Walk down the rows of magazine displays in the drugstore, and notice the periodicals that talk about fitness. Every month they offer regimens of improvement, work-out and diet schemes readers are invited to adopt. "Three sets, each with eight to twelve reps." "Twenty minutes, three or more times a week." "Upper body day, followed by lower body day, followed by full body day. And don't get them out of order!" "Double your protein, cut your carbos in half." "Eat five small meals, rather than three larger ones." "Breakfast like a king, lunch like a prince, supper like a pauper." How structured, how disciplined!

"Have you always been so disciplined about your health?" I asked my next door neighbor. I was coming home at the end of the day, and ran into him just as he was returning from his afternoon jog. We got to talking, and soon enough he was telling me the story of his commitment to fitness.

"Heck no, this hasn't always been my way. In fact, for most of my life, I avoided calisthenics and exercise like the plague. When people said I should limit myself to red meat once or twice a week and only drink on weekends, I laughed. When they tried to convince me to work out, I told them to get real. I believed human beings should flourish, and I thought that flourishing involved 'reaching for all the gusto you can get,' as the advertisement says.

"Oh, I did get some exercise. I got a bang out of skiing every winter, and tennis in the summer was fun. And I enjoy eating fish now and then, so my diet wasn't all that bad. But the beer at the end of the day was a non-negotiable. And a few snacks to go along! The result? I only grew somewhat fat. My blood pressure and cholesterol levels only rose somewhat. My physical fitness deteriorated only somewhat. And for a while that was good enough for me.

"Lately, though, it hasn't been good enough. I'm in the full throes of mid-life. My pace has slowed a bit, my memory's already starting to show signs of wear. I have half a closet full of clothes I can't fit in, and increasingly I pick my wardrobe for what it hides instead of what it reveals. And the last time I went for a physical, the doctor really gave me hell. I guess I'm coming to realize—perhaps I'm even starting to accept—that some plan of exercise and diet may be the only thing standing between me and death. And I don't want to die.

"So there it is: now there's a regular regimen of exercise in the rhythm of my daily life. Yuck!"

"Do you feel better?" I asked him.

"Not really," he answered. "But I still don't want to die." And I know what he means.

Discipline, the scholars say, is the ability to delay gratification for the sake of a long-term goal. Studying in order to graduate or pass an exam or get a job, training in order to win an athletic contest, postponing sexual release in order to increase the likelihood of conceiving—in so many areas of our lives, we're faced with the ugly, unavoidable prospect of discipline. And because we want to goal badly enough, we submit to the indignities it demands.

You can do anything, in other words, but you can't do everything. So we have to choose what we will do. We have to choose where we will go.

Discipline is about choosing what we'll do and where we'll go. It's also about choosing who we'll be. I must tell you a story from my own life.

It all began with my most recent attempt to quit smoking cigarettes. The attempt occurred about twenty years ago, but I remember that experience of quitting as if it just occurred.

As I imply, I'd tried to quit before—many times. This time, however, was different. What was the difference? It was this. This final time I didn't really change my behavior at all, what I changed was my personal identity.

In my previous attempts to quit, I now realize, I'd continued to see myself as a smoker; I just happened to be a smoker who didn't smoke. But that hadn't worked. Sooner or later the smoker in me would begin to reassert itself, and soon enough I'd be smoking again. For a behavior that's been stopped can just as easily be started again.

This time, however, I changed my identity. I accepted the sad but inescapable truth that I needed to become someone else if I wanted to live. I needed to become a former smoker.

I didn't like the prospect of being a former smoker. Most of the former smokers I knew were prissy and self-righteous people, and it brought me close to tears to think I should become one of them. At the same time, most of the continuing smokers I knew were lively, creative, free-living people. It broke my heart I could no longer say this of myself.

But unless I was willing to die, I realized, this is what had to happen: I needed to become someone else. And like my neighbor who gave in to the need to jog, I didn't want to die. So I accepted the pathetic but unavoidable fact that I was, in truth, a former smoker.

Strangely enough, this last attempt at quitting was in some ways the easiest of all my efforts. I wasn't tempted to smoke. (Former smokers don't smoke, after all.) I didn't feel anxiety, and there was very little tension in my life. In other ways, however, it was a terrible time. What I did feel was sadness. I was burying forever the person I'd been, a person I'd dearly loved. I resented that I had to do this. I raged against a world where it was impossible to smoke and live, and I raged against a God who allowed it to be so. The six months after I quit smoking were, on balance, among the worst times in my life, even though I was never tempted to smoke.

Yes, discipline is also about who we're going to be.

Scholars have found there's a profound, two-way relationship between what we do and who we are. If we want to train our children to live with honesty and compassion, for example, one part of the training is to insist they behave that way. We show them how to make concrete choices that are fair and gentle and good, and we make them face the fact that they have to choose the behaviors they want. But the other part of the training involves naming for the children the kind of person we're calling them to be, affirming that they're "good people, faithful and true."

And between these two parts of our training flows a powerful communication. On the one hand, we become the people implied by our acts. And on the other hand, we act in accord with the person we understand ourselves to be. Indeed, if anything, the second part is the more important.

It's about character, as many people are saying today. And they're right. In the end, wherever we look, whomever we observe, it's the choices that have been made that we notice. The choices about what to do, to be sure, but the choices about who to be, even more.

And that's what I learned, when the last cigarette was thrown away!

Why all this talk about physical fitness? What do my efforts to quit smoking have to do with becoming a spiritual person? The answer, you can see, is that what's true of our bodies is true of our spirits, as well. If it's true that without self-control my body will die from smoking, if it's true that without a regimen of exercise and diet our bodies will die from over-weight and under-strength, it's also true that without discipline our spirits will die from atrophy and waste. The fullness of personhood we want for ourselves will never come to be, and our spirits will never breathe fully, with joy and peace.

How can this be? How can discipline be so necessary, if the human journey is, in the end, nothing but a journey into the reality of who we are? And what sort of God is it, as I've asked before, who calls us to be our own fullest selves and then makes this something that's so unnatural to us that we have to structure the journey with rules? Surely the journey to ourselves, the journey to God, should come out of us spontaneously, characteristically, genuinely, with a facility that indicates now native it is to who we are. Doesn't this make sense?

Perhaps it does make sense. But at least one thing that argues in another direction must be noticed. And it's this. Every great religious tradition in the world has made a place for discipline.

Do Christians observe a lenten fast? Well, so also do Jews observe Yom Kippur. So also do Muslims observe Ramadan. So also do the monks of Buddhism and Hinduism and all the other great world religions have a time for sacrifice and self-denial. Are they all guilty of the same anti-worldly, bitter and suspicious view some of us once experienced? Or—heaven help us—have they all discovered a truth we sometimes avoid? I think it's the second.

And what's that truth? It's this. The fabric of the fully formed human person is only created by a weaving together that requires threads to be pulled and bent, dragged from their haughty autonomy into a beautiful, complementary tapestry. The human person is so complex that becoming our own fullest, best, most satisfying self is a struggle. It doesn't happen automatically; quite the contrary, it takes all the time and all the effort at our disposal. What's true of the body is also true of the soul. Achieving our natural health and wholeness does not, paradoxically, come naturally. On the contrary, flourishing as a human person demands a plan. It demands—oh, drats!— discipline.

Years ago I read a wonderful science fiction novel entitled *Time Enough for Love*. As I recall, it was about a time when science figured out a way for humans to live forever. For some reason only one person, a man, was given this gift. I don't recall if the scientists then somehow lost the ability to do this, or if better minds decided such a thing wasn't wise. In any case, only this one man had the gift of immortality.

In the novel the man has been alive for hundreds of years. He has buried many wives, has seen his children's children to several generations. He has, it seems, been everywhere, done everything. And thus the question arises for some of the other characters in the novel: does he regret having this gift of endless life?

The pivotal scene is burned in my memory. In response to their question, the man pauses thoughtfully, and then speaks his mind. "No," he says, "I don't regret it. The gift of endless life hasn't been without its sorrows, to be sure. And I have my days of anger or grief. But on balance I don't regret it. For this gift of long life has given me time enough to love.

"Loving isn't really an easy thing, after all, and it's taken me all these years, all these centuries, to learn how to do it. Now, I think I'm just about there. And as I look back, that's been worth all the prices I have paid. So, no, I don't regret a thing."

"For the longest time," the wise old man told me, "I couldn't figure out how to fit a period of reflection into my life. I tried all sorts of alternatives—when I first woke up, after work, in the midst of the evening. But nothing worked. No matter where I placed my quiet time, something inevitably intruded. The presence of my wife, the demands of the kids, the activities of my work—they all played their part in blocking my time for reflection. And I can't say I begrudged the intrusions of all these folks, either. I love my wife, after all. And I love my children and, indeed, my work. Still, the quiet time was missing. And I loved my quiet time, too.

"Little by little, an answer nibbled at my mind. I didn't really like the answer. I avoided it as long as I could, till I couldn't avoid it any more. But eventually its rightness just couldn't be ignored. If I really wanted this time of reflection, I'd need to find a time when no one else was around. And when was that time? Three A.M.! It's strange, I know. But I feel so much joy and peace, now that I get up every night in the middle of the night to spend my hour in personal reflection. I may be weird, but I'm also very happy."

I was stunned when I heard those words: a frightful discipline, smiling all the while!

When I hear these words, I'm reminded of Madeleine. A busy woman, with a successful career, she told me that whenever she's driving, she intentionally turns off the radio. She climbs inside the silence and allows it to climb inside her. Or, if she finds she's just too distracted to focus, she puts on a tape of inspirational music. The silence and the songs raise her spirit, they give her life.

I'm reminded of a monk who told me: "Most people find it hard to pray because they feel distracted by all the activities of their life, by their so-called 'worldly concerns.' But that simply shows they understand prayer as some esoteric activity, and it's not. Prayer is really just the profoundly human activity of disciplined attention. Attention to what? Why, to everything! And perhaps most of all to those everyday experiences. I tell people to pray their experiences, to see those experiences not as distractions but as prayer's natural focus.

"The only thing, though— the trick, if you will—is to consider our experiences not as problems to be solved but as wonders to be contemplated. Don't spend prayer time figuring out how to make enough money to pay the Visa bill. Spend prayer time figuring out what it means that there's not enough money to pay the Visa bill and that paying it off is important and that we keep buying things we don't really need."

I'm reminded of a woman, a scholar with a lively career and a productive life, who once announced: "To be a spiritual person, you need only one discipline. You need the discipline of awareness. It's amazing how unaware we human persons can be. And without discipline you cannot become aware. But if you structure into your life a time and a place and a method for awareness, you'll be fine."

And what's involved in this awareness? She was clear about that, too. "Awareness involves looking while suspending judgment. You'll be surprised how hard it is not to immediately label everything good or bad, success or failure. Instead, suspend those judgments and just look. From what you see you'll learn. From what you learn you'll grow. And that's what it's all about."

"No pain, no gain," the coach said. He always struck me as a tad sadistic! But he was also speaking a truth. Muscles shout as they grow, they yelp as they become strong. But the result is that they become fluid and frisky, able and alive.

The same is true of our deeper selves, our most human selves. Our spirits need to grow to be fully alive. And growth, of any kind, takes work, takes effort, takes a plan. It takes, in the end, discipline.

I don't like this fact. But it's a fact nonetheless. And unless this fact be included here, I fear this book would lie to you. Just as we would not die, so we must not lie.

For it's truth, and truth alone, that will set our spirits free. It's truth that will let our spirits breathe. It's truth that will show us how to live with joy and peace.

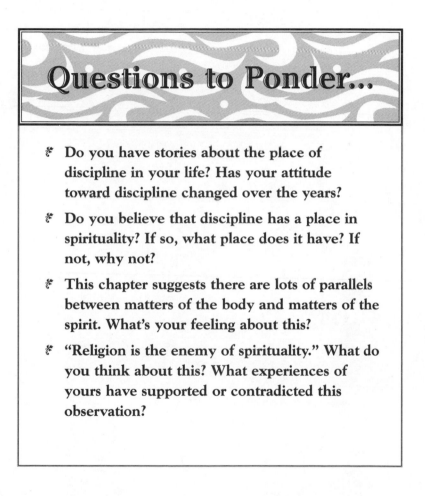

Questions to Ponder...

❦ Do you have stories about the place of discipline in your life? Has your attitude toward discipline changed over the years?

❦ Do you believe that discipline has a place in spirituality? If so, what place does it have? If not, why not?

❦ This chapter suggests there are lots of parallels between matters of the body and matters of the spirit. What's your feeling about this?

❦ "Religion is the enemy of spirituality." What do you think about this? What experiences of yours have supported or contradicted this observation?

ARM IN ARM

Don and his three colleagues were strolling the aisles of the department store, singing the various holiday carols as they'd been hired to do. Wrapped in colorful scarves, jaunty caps on their heads, they gave a wondrously festive feel to the bustle of the shopping experience. The fact that they were very talented musicians, blending their beautiful voices into rich and intriguing harmonies, only made it better.

They came, in due course, to the cosmetics department. Don caught the eye of a small Asian saleswoman. "Do you sing 'Silent Night'?" she quietly asked. Of course they did. The group started their rendition, focusing on the special nuances they'd so carefully developed.

Suddenly another sound! Don looked. The saleswoman was singing. A sweet, clear sound. A beautiful, clear soprano voice. But what words? Suddenly, it became clear: she was singing the ancient, traditional carol in Korean.

The group leader looked at Don and the others, gave a subtle signal. The quartet stopped singing the words, switching instead to a soft, rich humming sound. And after the briefest shy hesitation, the saleswoman accepted her role and gave herself to the song. Together they soared on the wings of the tune and of its gentle, supportive harmony.

People turned. Shoppers stopped. A hush fell over the department. The song claimed the space and the moment—and their hearts. The little group of five followed their music to its peak and then slowly, gently down to its chord of rest. "Sleep in heavenly peace." A silence, a shared and cherished silence. And then applause that rolled through the store, up and down the aisles, that enveloped the singers in love, returning to them the gift they'd created for all to enjoy.

Don told me he had tears in his eyes at the end. And he wasn't the only one. For there, in the unlikely setting of a department store, one of life's important lessons had been made clear. In the quest to live with joy and peace, we can only go part-way by ourselves. But together, arm in arm, we can achieve the dreams of our spirit. And when that happens, what beautiful music we make!

Stephanie and Carl know the truth of this lesson. They'd waited so long for their baby. The process of adoption seemed endless, and the fact that this was their second child only made things worse. But at last they'd welcomed their little bundle of joy, a tiny baby girl given into their safe-keeping and love.

Stephanie's a dancer and a teacher of ballet. She wanted to keep working, at least for a while; and there seemed no reason not to. Of course, it took some thinking to figure out what to do with the baby. But then a wondrous idea struck her. The staff at the adoption agency had urged her to provide the baby as much physical contact as possible. Especially with adopted babies, they said, it's important to help the process of bonding between mother and child in any way you can. So Stephanie suddenly realized just what she'd do.

She arrived a little early for dance class, her baby in her arms. As the time approached, she changed into her leotards. Then, taking a long, wide strip of cloth, she gently bound her baby to her chest. Round and round she wound the cloth, until the baby was safe and secure, tucked against her mother's breast, her ear perfectly placed to hear the reassuring beat of her mother's heart.

In this position, then, Stephanie proceeded to dance. Arm in arm with her baby she danced. And oh, did her mother's heart fly, right along with her dancer's body.

❦

In these pages we've been talking about our desire to heal our restless hearts with a personal spirituality. But precisely because our goal's been a spirituality that's personal, that nurtures the flourishing of our individual spirits into a life of joy and peace, a danger is that the project can become terribly self-centered. We can begin to view other people—either individual people or that gathering of people called the community—as the enemy of our individual flourishing.

But that's not the case. Indeed, the human spirit only flourishes in the midst of kindred spirits. We wend our way to our full humanity only when we walk arm in arm.

I think it's hard for every human being to fully appreciate how true this is, this interdependence that marks our human journey. But the fact is that the temptation to separate ourselves from our neighbors, to view our individual growth as competing with the demands of community, this is an especially American temptation. And so I think we should give it more than passing attention.

There's hardly anything more characteristic of Americans, after all, than our love of freedom. We value freedom perhaps more than any other gift of citizenship, and there are many good reasons why we should. It has provided us the means for the achievement of many human dreams and has been, through us, a gift to the whole of humankind. But many scholars believe our love of freedom, as beautiful as it is, can still become our undoing. And when does that happen? When it degenerates into the evil triplets: individualism, consumerism, and violence. Let me explain.

For example, it's so easy for us to understand freedom as nothing else than individual license, as my right to do whatever I want and your responsibility to stay the heck out of my way! We can be tempted to see everything and everyone outside of ourselves as the enemy. Whether it's the activities of government structuring society for the common good, or the needs of my family and friends, my neighbors and colleagues—I can be tempted to view all of it as enemy. And when I do that, I give in to the evil fallacy called individualism.

So, one of our particular American curses is that our concern to maximize the (very real) good of individual freedom can lead us to lose the very thing we need in order to achieve the (even more important) good of individual fulfillment. And why are we tempted to this curse? The answer lies in the second of the evil triplets. It goes by the name of "consumerism," and what I'm talking about is our addiction to things in preference to people.

For many of us, our lives are filled with things we don't really need. They're nice things, to be sure; many of them are useful, some of them are delightful. But few of them are absolutely necessary. And why do we covet these things so much? Some will answer that the culprit is advertising. But more deeply, the culprit is an overall environment, as near and as invisible as the air we breathe. This environment focuses our attention on things. It tells us that things measure our worth as persons. It invites us to evaluate the success of our lives by the things we have. And it urges us to protect our things at whatever cost, for losing them is losing the very essence of the life we cherish. We breathe this air called consumerism; it infects us. Often enough it holds us in a thrall that can be called addiction.

But that's not the worst of it. Individualism might be a harmless fallacy, consumerism might be a modest addiction. But mix them together, make them face the fact that other people are around, individuals like us, who may want the things we have—and violence inevitably follows. Indeed, wars are almost always fought over things, protecting them or trying to acquire them.

To a frightening degree, violence is a triplet never far behind its siblings, individualism and consumerism. In fact, we can picture these three as points on an endless triangle. Each leads to the others, all of them interconnect. And together, they wreak havoc with our dreams of a life lived with joy and peace. They guarantee our spirits can never freely breathe.

Is there hope? Of course there is. This whole book offers words of hope. Here let me simply say that since the destructive triangle of the evil triplets can be started anywhere, it can also be broken anywhere. Opt for peace instead of violence. Choose to live for people instead of things, with simplicity instead of ostentation. And most particularly work to replace antagonism with alliance, competition with compassion.

Do this, and hope will quickly follow.

❧❧

When I was in graduate school in New York, I got to know a young man who lived upstairs in the same building. His parents' home was not far away, in Brooklyn, but it was too far to commute each day. So he lived at our rooming house during the week, returning to his parents' home each weekend. One weekend John invited me to come to Sunday dinner.

John's ethnic heritage was Italian. Although his family was in many ways utterly Americanized, they still cherished some powerful Italian traditions. Perhaps foremost among those traditions, I discovered, was the Sunday dinner.

We began at one o'clock in the afternoon, and finished at seven in the evening. During that time we never stopped eating, though always at a leisurely pace and in amazingly moderate amounts. The food was wonderful. The table arrangements were gracious and beautiful. But what I most remember now, twenty years later, was the conversations of that meal.

John's mother would serve one of the courses of the meal. We'd enjoy the food, savoring it slowly and praising the cook. Then we'd be done, proud of our empty plates. I expected the dishes to be removed. But no, the conversation would continue, comfortably, for another fifteen or twenty minutes. Eventually John's mother would judge the moment to proceed had come. She'd rise, begin the clearing of the plates, and move on to the next course.

And what did they talk about in those intervals? Absolutely everything. They asked about me and my work. They seemed truly interested. They tarried over the details I shared, remarked on them, asked more, offered compliments and comments. They talked about themselves, telling me as much as I wanted to know, answering my interested questions and enjoying my sincere responses. One by one the parents turned to each of their children. They inquired how the week had gone in school, about progress on the sports teams, about their various friends. And these were not quick, perfunctory questions. They were extended conversations in which each child in turn was the friendly and loving focus of attention.

In the end, every person around that table felt heard. Each one of us become known in amazing detail and appreciated in very specific and pertinent ways. These individuals reestablished themselves as a family through that meal. And to a memorable degree I became part of their family. Welcomed sincerely, embraced enthusiastically, loved genuinely, I shared in the beauty and the love that made this family real.

We were arm in arm by the end of the day. As I drove home I felt privileged. I had the suspicion I'd never forget that dinner. And I never have.

The customs of that wonderful Italian-American family are not my customs, at least not entirely. But I've had the chance to express my own variation on the theme of mealtime sharing, a variation rooted in my own history as well as in theirs.

Some months ago a group of us were gathered for Thanksgiving Day. It was the first time in my life I'd hosted this annual gathering. For once, I hadn't traveled to my relatives in another state. Instead, a local gathering had been arranged—one of those fascinating gatherings where one person invites another, who in turn knows of someone else who's looking for a place to go. The result was seven people, no one of whom knew everyone before they gathered around this table.

We'd taken our places. The food had been placed before us. And then it was time to give thanks. My mind went back to my own childhood. In my family, it was customary to pray a grace before every meal; but through the months of the year, a formal, memorized text was always used. Except for once. On Thanksgiving Day my father annually mustered the courage and conviction to speak in his own words a prayer of thanks. He'd refer to the high points of the year. He'd acknowledge the moments of stress or suffering. And he'd celebrate that we were still together, still seeking to love, still trying to be worthy of the gifts we'd received. For this he'd give thanks. And in response we'd all say "Amen."

My mind went back to those Thanksgiving Days of my childhood. I was struck by the beauty of my father's tradition. And so I opened my mouth to pray.

I noted that we all came from different families, that our love felt stronger pulls to people far away than to one another. But I offered the thought that this only brought into our room, around our table, a great, huge, wonderful group of people, gathered here on the wings of our thoughts and imaginations. I gave thanks for all those relatives and friends. I celebrated the serendipitous way that we seven had come to be a community of thanks and the small but valuable gift we'd become to one another. I acknowledged the gifts that had come to each of us—and to those we loved—in the past year. For all of this I sincerely prayed with thanks. And all those around the table answered with an "Amen" that was just as sincere.

There we were, arm in arm, hand in hand. And I, for one, felt wonderfully blessed.

∽∽∾∾

Talking about important stuff is tough. Sometimes it's that we don't quite know what we think, and in our confusion we can't find anything to say. Other times it's that we fear we'll be ridiculed if we speak our thoughts, and so we keep silent. But one way or another, we human beings have a tough time talking about what's really important. It's no surprise, then, that people have a hard time talking about their heart's deepest desire, about the yearnings of their spirit for full and expressive life. As one friend of mine said, "If I brought this stuff up with most of my friends, they'd think I was nuts!"

But if it's true that we achieve our goals only when we walk arm in arm, it's especially true that we need to share these yearnings, to explore with others the questions about life that most deeply, importantly plague us. That's why, through much of human history, there's been a special role for people who are good at listening to our mumblings on these important topics. Such people have been called spiritual guides or spiritual companions, sometimes gurus or mentors. I call them "soul friends," and I think we all need them.

Is there a soul friend in your life? Don't be too quick to say there's not. Such people don't come with academic credentials. They don't have diplomas on the wall or name plates on the door, so they may not be easy to notice. Is there a woman across the alley, with whom you enjoy sharing a cup of coffee, spending time that tends to turn to really important things? Is there a colleague at the office who tends to stop by your desk— or you stop by theirs—when there's no immediate pressing business to conduct? Is there a friend from long ago, someone you've stayed in touch with for no particular reason, whose occasional visits always end up in wonderful conversations that last long into the night? If there is, then you may well have a soul friend.

And if not . . . well, then, you need one. Look around, see if there's someone in your life whose wisdom you appreciate, whose judgment you trust, whose experience seems to enrich your own life's journey. Cultivate such people, let them become soul friends, if they will. There's no need to give it a name, to make it a formal thing. Just let the relationship grow. And allow the conversation to move to deeper levels.

Or seek out someone who's taken intentional, diligent steps to become a good soul friend. I've said that soul friends don't need academic degrees. But it's also true that some people so enjoy being a companion on the journey that they prepare themselves to do this work well. They study and practice to improve their ability to hear what you say. They deeply explore their own experience to be sure they won't complicate your journey with mere prejudices of their own. They arrange to have their work supervised by someone even more experienced, to be sure they don't compromise their relationship with you by acting on their own needs when they're supposed to be trying to meet yours.

There are many such people, good and holy, wise and experienced. They're found in the ranks of the clergy of various traditions. They're located among the numbers of counselors, social workers, teachers. You hear about them from others who've found them helpful. You meet them and feel a positive chemistry in your conversation. One way or another you get the sense that this person could be a soul friend to you. Act on your intuition, trust the judgment of your heart.

We walk arm in arm on the journey to a life of joy and peace. But that doesn't mean we always split the load half-and-half. In the luck of life, we've been fed by many people we've never had a chance to thank. In response, we try to offer help to others, without worrying about what we'll get back in return for our gifts. Arm in arm, sometimes we're the guide, sometimes we're the person being guided. Sometimes we take the lead, and sometimes we're content to safely follow. Sometimes we benefit from the wisdom of a soul friend. And someday—who knows—someone will find us just the soul friend they need.

All of this shows us journeying arm in arm, just as people should.

≈≈

Just a few weeks ago there was an article in the newspaper reporting a most amazing development. It seems that on many college campuses there's been a giant burst of popularity in ballroom dancing. Why is this? It's certainly not the need for exercise, and it isn't any naive expectation of becoming Ginger Rogers or Fred Astaire. No, it's something else—and something much more important. It's the need for human intimacy, physical and emotional at once, safe and still deeply satisfying.

We live in a time when sexual activity seems to be more pervasive than ever, casual and uncommitted, and many people seem to think that's great. But it's also a problem, no matter what one's moral views. For one thing, achieving physical intimacy is no guarantee that true interpersonal connection will follow. The sad jokes about people who had sex and then forgot the partner's name give evidence that these two don't always go together. And for another thing, people who don't want to be sexually active often find themselves tragically blocked from any physical connection at all. Teachers are instructed never to touch their students lest sexual innuendo be perceived. Friends and neighbors carefully contain their gestures lest there be any miscommunication. The result is an odd, pathetic paradox: we're an over sexualized and yet touch-deprived culture!

This is the need to which ballroom dancing responds. You can't do the waltz without touching your partner. So one of the pleasures of couple-dancing is the way two bodies get to hold each other. At the same time, the "rules" of the touching are clear and known by all involved. Only certain kinds of touch are proper. And when the music ends, the touching will also cease. So it's a safe kind of touching. No one need fear that it will be infected with misinterpretation or tumble terrifyingly out of control. It will be what it is and nothing more, and thus it can be enjoyed with confidence and comfort. No wonder ballroom dancing's popular!

Even for those of us who have no sense of rhythm, the need to dance is real. Arm in arm we need to dance with our families and friends, with the elders who show us the way and the children whose future we serve. We need to touch one another, body and soul. With sincerity and safety, with respect and reverence we need to hold one another, helping one another to be strong and assuring one another of dependable support. We need to allow a soul friend to lead us around the dance floor of life, being content with the role of follower no matter what our gender. And in the same way, we must be prepared to take the lead, when another dancer asks us to show them the way.

Yes, in our bodies and in our spirits we need to dance, and in the dance we need to proclaim a powerful truth. Our flourishing as human persons happens together or it never happens at all. We are kindred spirits. We walk arm in arm— we dance arm in arm—on our human journey. Arm in arm, and only in this way, will our spirits learn to breathe.

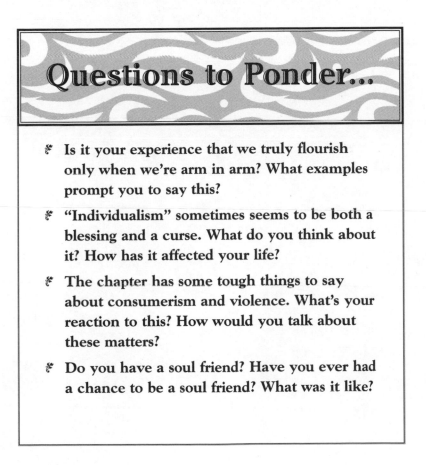

Questions to Ponder...

❀ Is it your experience that we truly flourish only when we're arm in arm? What examples prompt you to say this?

❀ "Individualism" sometimes seems to be both a blessing and a curse. What do you think about it? How has it affected your life?

❀ The chapter has some tough things to say about consumerism and violence. What's your reaction to this? How would you talk about these matters?

❀ Do you have a soul friend? Have you ever had a chance to be a soul friend? What was it like?

LETTING GO

My good friend Marty died last week. Any death prompts sadness, of course, as we feel the absence of someone we love. But this was all the more sad since Marty was only forty-six years old and the death was sudden.

Actually, Marty's struggle with health wasn't new. Almost twenty years ago he was in an automobile accident. Spinal injury resulted, and it took him a couple of years of therapy to get to the point of walking with crutches. But Marty's will was strong. He stuck with his regimen of physical therapy, learned to drive a car with hand controls, and returned to his professional life with vigor and skill. In fact, Marty saw his condition as a tolerable inconvenience. "This isn't so bad," he said. "What I couldn't stand would be to be bound to a wheelchair."

He spoke too soon. About five years ago, his condition deteriorated. A tremendous flare-up of pain put Marty back in the hospital. Treatment eventually managed to contain the pain, but years of strain had made the spinal injury worse. When the whole episode was over, Marty was in that wheelchair for good.

I think it surprised even him that Marty found the strength to move on. But he did. He went back to the rehab center and learned to handle the range of daily tasks in a new way. Eventually he was able to move into his own home. For a while, he needed a live-in companion to help him get around. But finally, in a move he was very proud of, Marty began to live on his own once again. He figured out how to get himself and his wheelchair into the car, went back to work part-time, and rejoined the human community with a vengeance.

Pain was never far away for Marty. For years, when we went out to dinner, we had to schedule things so he could take his evening pain medication on time and be home in bed when it took full effect. It was the only way he could get a night's sleep. Now, as I've come to understand it, all this medicating had a cost. While Marty's spinal injury was so profoundly disturbing his everyday life, the various chemicals he needed were quietly doing their own damage, putting a cumulative strain on his heart. And eventually the daily regimen took its toll.

They found Marty, fully dressed, sitting in his wheelchair in front of the TV, dead of a heart attack. He'd let go of walking unimpeded and then of walking at all. He'd let go of full-time work and of a day without pain. In the end, last week, Marty let go of life.

Letting go—that's what it's all about. That, in the end, is the real key to letting our spirits breathe.

For Christians, the center of their faith is the event of Jesus' death and rising to new life. Each year they tell again the story of his final days, marking his actions in a journey from Holy Thursday through Good Friday to Easter Sunday. And as they do so, Christians struggle to wrap their minds around one of life's most profound truths: living fully, living with joy and peace, is finally grounded on the act of letting go, moving through death to life.

Christians believe Jesus saved the whole human family in his act of love, as he accepted the price of his fidelity and embraced the world's fate for him. In a classic formulation in the Christian scriptures, Paul's Letter to the Philippians proclaims that Jesus "did not regard equality with God as something to be exploited, but emptied himself, taking the form of a slave, being born in human likeness. And being found in human form, he humbled himself and became obedient to the point of death–even death on a cross." (Philippians 2:6–8) So letting go is at the heart of what Jesus did for the human family–letting go first of his divinity and then of his very humanity out of love.

And it isn't just Christians who appreciate this sense of the challenge of letting go. Many of the great religious traditions see this truth. At the heart of the Jewish tradition, for example, is the notion that embracing the law (torah) is really embracing freedom, as one abandons autonomy in favor of

covenant relationship with God. And the weekly celebration
of Sabbath, where endless work is replaced by a spirit of leisure
made possible only by trust in the divine, becomes a recurring
declaration of the power of letting go. Similarly, followers of
the Buddha struggle to achieve a spirit of resignation which will
open them to universal compassion, a sense of oneness that
comes from a willingness to protect nothing of oneself. And for
Muslims, trust in the kindness of Allah is so complete that, as
one scholar said, "Islam is not part of life, Islam is life."

So here's a lesson that's pointed at all of us. Time and again
through our lives, we're tempted to grab onto something, to hold
it as if it will take care of us forever. But nothing can fill that
role. And so we need to learn to let go, to stop our grasping.

The speaker was a sharp, savvy old man. For years he'd run a
half-way house for recovering alcoholics, and now he was being
honored for his work. In the midst of his words of thanks, he
made a comment that's remained with me ever since. And the
fact that he was himself a recovering alcoholic only made his
sassy metaphor more wonderful. "Life," he said, "is like an ice
cube. You've got two choices. You can try to hold onto it,
squeezing it in your hand. Then, of course, it does nothing but
melt and mess up your clothes and dribble uselessly away. Or
you can give it away, letting it drop into your favorite drink. It's
still gone, of course. But the result is a hell of a lot more tasty!"

Yes, time and again we need to learn this lesson. Isn't it
amazing the way we're constantly tempted to grasp things, in
the vain hope we can stop life's truest process? It can be

money. "What are you saving it for?" shouted the preacher. "You can't take it with you!" It can be prestige. The terrible blow experienced by people who lose their jobs really isn't about income; it's about self-esteem. How difficult it is to remember that our value isn't based on external signs of success. It can be relationships. "Why are you still dating that guy," her brother asked her, "he's a loser!" She started to cry, and her unnervingly honest reply slipped out. "If I didn't have him, I wouldn't have anybody!" I think most of us can identify with her feelings.

Years ago I read a book about the challenges of living that included a powerful line: "It takes sixty years to make a human person. And when the process is done, the person is ready for the one act that's really important: dying." It was a disturbing statement, in some ways very negative. But as I've lived, I've become convinced it was wise and true. The little challenges that keep coming at us in life are really rehearsals for the real and final challenge.

Time and again we're tempted to hold on to something or someone, in the vain attempt to engineer immortality. Hopefully we overcome the temptation. Or at least, when life rips away some valued possession despite our efforts, hopefully we're wise enough to learn from the experience. In either case, if we're lucky the truth becomes little by little clearer: that real life is found in letting go, and so we grow and deepen and begin to experience the joy and peace for which we yearn. For if this is how things go, then when the final test comes our way we'll find within ourselves the strength to embrace our true reality. We'll let go fully, finally, ultimately. We'll die— and then we'll live.

We yearn to have spirits that breathe. But breathing involves two movements: sucking in and expelling out, gathering and releasing. The person who's afraid to release will never breathe. And such a person will surely die. The person who has the courage to expel the old air, on the other hand, trusting that new, fresh air will somehow arrive, will survive and flourish. And such a person can live forever.

On Good Friday, Christians retell the story of Jesus' final hours. Jesus is betrayed, is beaten up, and then is condemned. He's forced to carry the instrument of his own death to the place of execution. His clothes are stolen and then divvied up. He's mocked, ignored, abused. Finally, the moment of death approaches. According to the Christian scriptures, Jesus speaks out. "Father, forgive them; for they do not know what they are doing." (Luke 23:34) And then, "it is finished." (John 19:30)

"My friend Gail and I had a terrible fight," the young woman, a student of mine, told me. "It started as an argument about boys, but then it escalated. We both said things that were mean and nasty. She hurt me terribly, and I know I hurt her, too. I wanted to. When I couldn't take it any more, I ran away, out of the student union and back to the dorm. I rushed into my room. I slammed the door behind me, threw off my coat, fell on the bed, and sobbed.

"Then I heard a soft knock on the door. 'Sherry, please let me in. Can't we talk?'

"I didn't let her in. It's one of the most awful things I've ever done, in my whole life. But I just couldn't forgive her; and I knew if I let her in, I'd have to. At last she walked away. I just lay there. I hated her, and I hated myself. And I couldn't do anything. I just cried and cried."

Life's ultimate challenge is the challenge of letting go. You'd think the easiest thing to let go of would be guilt and anger. Who would want to hurt, when the path to happiness is so near at hand? But that's not the way it is. For some strange and mysterious reason, the letting go we find the hardest is the letting go that comes from forgiveness.

All of us are hurt by life, and so all of us face the challenge of forgiving the cause of our hurts. Why should we forgive? In many cases, I suspect, the truth is that those who hurt us "don't know what they are doing." And that's certainly a good reason to forgive them. But in other cases, the truth is that they know exactly what they're doing. Even here, though, we ought to forgive. For until we forgive, we're trapped, owned by the anger and the pain, weighed down by a past that won't go away because we won't let it go. Paradoxically, then, as we hold on to the anger as if it's our possession, it ends up possessing us, and we're enslaved to the hurts we won't release.

Letting go—that's what it's all about. And forgiving the folks who hurt us along the way is a big part of letting go.

And now we come to the deepest, most challenging truth about forgiveness. About a hundred years ago, a young French girl named Thérèse of Lisieux entered a convent. Her health wasn't good, and she died in 1897, at the age of twenty-four. But her heroism is such that the Catholic church considers her a saint. Thérèse is commonly known as the Little Flower; and, to tell the truth, her life is often romanticized in an appalling way. But this young woman was no fool. And as she wrestled with the challenges that came her way in her short life, she became not only holy but also wise.

I think one of Thérèse's wisest insights occurred when she made the following statement: "If you are willing to bear serenely the trial of being displeasing to yourself, then you will be for Jesus a pleasant place of shelter." I realize the language and perspective of this statement are in some ways quaint. But I still find great wisdom in her challenge to "bear serenely the trial of being displeasing to yourself." To accept with equanimity our own imperfections. Not to become blasé about the ways in which we hurt those we love, of course. Surely we try to love well the ones that are near and dear to us. But also to remain peaceful about the inevitable truth of our own flaws. To forgive, and to include in our forgiveness even ourselves. To let go, and to let go not only of our anger against others but also our hate or disdain for ourselves. What a wonderful thing!

That our spirits may breathe, we have to let go. That we may live with joy and peace, we have to let go. To befriend our fellow travelers on life's journey, we have to let go. And to walk peacefully with ourselves, we have to let go.

In her letting go of us, our mothers birthed us into the life we now know. In our own letting go, and only then, will we birth ourselves to the life for which we never cease to yearn.

In 1982, one of the most wonderful movies ever made, *E.T.: The Extraterrestrial*, appeared. The story's well known. I hope you've seen the movie, and can picture the scenes I recall.

Early in the movie, the little boy Elliott discovers E.T., hiding in the garden shed. He tempts E.T. into the house and hides him in the bedroom closet. He tries to keep a secret, but he can't. So eventually he drags his older brother and little sister into the room and shows them his new friend. And Elliott tells them his plan. "I'm going to keep him," he says. Elliott is little, and he doesn't understand. So he can't resist the urge to hold on to what he has.

In the middle of the movie, there's a scene in which Elliott cuts his finger; "Ouch," he says automatically. E.T. reaches out with his own glowing finger, touches Elliott's finger, and heals the wound. And through successive scenes like this, we watch as the two of them grow closer and closer to each other, developing a bond that can only be called love.

E.T. starts to fail, of course. This world is not his home, and he's not suited to survive here. The authorities intervene. They may be grown-ups, but they understand even less than Elliott. They desperately try to own and control and hang on to E.T. But it can't be done. And in that heart-breaking scene,

E.T. appears to die as Elliott watches on, helplessly, from his bed near by. But no, E.T. is not dead. His wondrous heart starts to beat again, and to glow with life. Is there some scientific reason for his renewed vigor? Or has Elliott's love given him life? Who knows?

Now, comes the moment of truth. If E.T. is to live, he must go to the world for which he's suited. And if Elliott really wants E.T. to live, he must let him go. All this Elliott comes to understand, with a wisdom far beyond his years, a wisdom to which we devote a lifetime's search. And so Elliott and his friends smuggle E.T. onto their bikes and rush, race, fly toward the site where contact can finally be made.

The space ship arrives. The door opens. The moment of separation arrives. E.T. and Elliott look at each other. E.T. takes that gentle, powerful finger of his, that finger that glows and heals, and points at his own heart. "Ouch," he says, in a communication that expresses it all. "Ouch."

Elliott and E.T. touch one last time, and then Elliott, bravely, beautifully, amazingly, lets him go. Suddenly E.T.'s heart glows bright and warm, living and strong. He points at his heart once again. Then he points upward, leading Elliott's eyes skyward.

"I'll be right here," he says. "I'll be right here." He turns and hobbles into the waiting space craft.

The center of E.T. is his heart. It is the heart's energy that flows into his primitive words and his powerful gestures. It is the heart's life that pulses forth through his finger, sending healing and health to those around.

It's a restless heart, this heart of E.T. And like our restless hearts, it yearns for home. But it's also a heart in contact with other hearts, sensitive and sharing, loving and truly alive. It's a heart that must come to grips with letting go; there's no denying that. But more profoundly it's a heart that knows how letting go actually transforms separation into a new form of presence, how dying leads to full and endless life.

Our spirits yearn to breathe. Our hearts yearn for a life of joy and peace. What does it look like when this goal is achieved? What does it look like when our restless hearts have finally learned how to rest? What does it look like when the journey of our spirits—the journey that's occupied us through the many pages of this book—has finally come to a glorious, victorious end?

It looks like this.

"I'll be right here. I'll be right here."

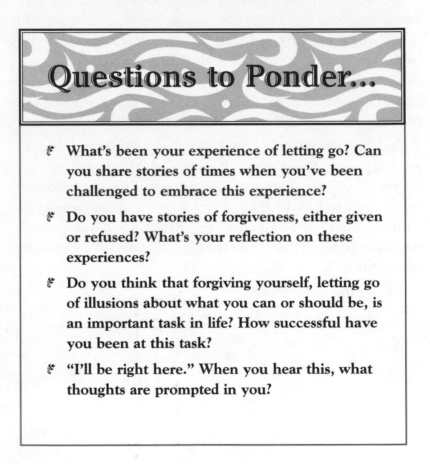

Questions to Ponder...

❧ What's been your experience of letting go? Can you share stories of times when you've been challenged to embrace this experience?

❧ Do you have stories of forgiveness, either given or refused? What's your reflection on these experiences?

❧ Do you think that forgiving yourself, letting go of illusions about what you can or should be, is an important task in life? How successful have you been at this task?

❧ "I'll be right here." When you hear this, what thoughts are prompted in you?

TIMOTHY E. O'CONNELL, PH.D., is a professor of pastoral studies at Loyola University in Chicago. A widely known author and speaker, Dr. O'Connell is also the author of *Tend Your Own Garden: How to Raise Great Kids*, and *Good People, Tough Choices: Making the Right Decisions Every Day*, also published by Thomas More. Future books will continue to address the challenges of living in the world today.

Timothy O'Connell welcomes the reflections of his readers. You may contact him by mail at:

> Institute of Pastoral Studies
> Loyola University Chicago
> 6525 N. Sheridan Road
> Chicago, IL 60626

You may also contact him by e-mail at:

> toconne@luc.edu

To learn more about Dr. O'Connell's upcoming projects and appearances, and to pursue the subjects of his books, we invite you to visit his web site:

> www.timoconnell.com